Uncertainty: The Painful Experience

OrangeBooks Publication

1st Floor, Rajhans Arcade, Mall Road, Kohka, Bhilai, Chhattisgarh 490020
Website: **www.orangebooks.in**

© Copyright, 2024, Author

All rights reserved. No part of this book may be reproduced, stored in a retrieval system, or transmitted, in any form by any means, electronic, mechanical, magnetic, optical, chemical, manual, photocopying, recording or otherwise, without the prior written consent of its writer.

First Edition, 2024

ISBN: 978-93-6554-051-2

UNCERTAINTY
The Painful Experience

PRIYANKA UPADHYAY

OrangeBooks Publication
www.orangebooks.in

Preface

This is my first book based on my experience as a parent, when your small and only child and you yourself is going through hard phases of life. I am writing our journey, the experiences we had. Through this book I want to convey to all of you that "no matter whatever hard/tough time life gives you; you should always be a warrior and fight with it". My child is undergoing treatment of one of the dangerous diseases which I want everyone to know so if anyone see any such symptoms, they can take proactive measures and can contact the doctors. When you have lot of emotions inside you and you can't convey to anyone, a book will help you to release your stress. I have put all my emotions, my feelings, what we have experienced inside the book.

I dedicate this book to all the parents who are holding a big smile on their face, but crying deeply inside their heart for someone they lost, or for someone undergoing some major treatment or serious illness. We all are worried for this uncertainty of life which leaves behind sorrows and sadness. But the good thing is for certain diseases, our medical science have done lot of drastic advancements. I request all parents to just keep in mind "All is well" and nothing can hamper their happiness.

I know saying thanks to your parents is difficult. If I go and say thanks to my parents they will say "please no formalities, it's our duty. Who say thanks to parents and all!!"

But the way they supported us during our one of the most difficult time, nobody else in a relation will ever do. Somewhere I read "One of the greatest titles in the world is 'parent,' and one of the biggest blessings in the world is to have parents to call mom and dad." And I have felt every bit of it. I want to thank my father, my mother, my mother-in law and father-in law who supported us in crucial times when needed the most. I also want to thank my family, friends, relatives who helped us in different ways, sometimes it was a phone call to keep us positive and sometimes visiting us and making us happy.

I also wanted to thank my office boss, who always supported me. I have never seen a boss like him before, whenever it comes to family, he advises us to take care of family first and office work the second priority. Whenever I need any advice or facing any challenges in office/work, I just message him and whenever he gets time, he responds, though he is many levels upper than me, but no ego at all. But due to some unfortunate incident, he lost his only child and this incident have affected me so much that I don't have any words to say.

"Thank you"

About Me

My name is Priyanka, was born in a small town Obra Sone Bhadra, UP. I am sure nobody knows this place :D.

I am forth and the youngest child of my parents. Things were going good with me but when I was in class 7th, I was diagnosed with a disease called "Tuberculosis". Tuberculosis is the second deadly disease after cancer, so you can call me a TB survivor. I was so mature enough at the age of 12, was so eager to live my life that I never missed a single dose of tablet while going through drug therapy for 9 months. I think people born during 80's to 95's were more matured and responsible before their age as compared to people who are born after 95's. It's just an assumption I have, I am not comparing GenZ and millennials. My drug therapy for TB started in Jan 2002 and it got ended in Sep 2002 and finally doctor told my parents not to worry as I am fully cured. My weight also gained. Before TB diagnosis it was 27 kg at the age of 12 years, after the treatment it was 39 kg which showed a good progress and things started going good after that.

In 2015, I got married to my college batchmate, we did B.Tech from HMFA college located in Handia, Allahabad. Since we were from same religion and castes, there was not much issue with the marriage, the only concern was we were from two different states, UP and Bihar.

23-April 2018
Arjun Born

Me and my husband was from same college and fortunate enough to work in same organization. "Amdocs" which came as a boon to us as there was so much flexibility in our organization and we spent most of our time in organization only, so basically most of the pregnancy time were spent in Amdocs.

I was so glad that my teammates were so good not one or two, but the entire team including my team leader and managers. All were very friendly. My pregnancy was an adventure to them, as they were mostly unmarried and those who were married were recently married. All of them always gather around me and then ask me about my feelings, they always supported and helped me, always asking if you need anything from canteen let us know we will bring. It was really a very beautiful feeling.

Since I was having nausea during my first trimester, my boss adviced everyone on the floor not to have non-veg food, onion or garlic food because these causes vomiting to me and all the people followed his adviced till 9 months. I was blessed to be part of such team.

One of the best things in Amdocs is you can take your kids along with you and can work also.

So, with the happy journey of my 9 months pregnancy, the most awaiting day came. Before this pregnancy, I had two miscarriages. And this time it was a healthy baby with 3.6 kg weight, our joy was having no bound at all. We were lucky enough that during these days my mother, father, Father-in-law, mother-in-law, my brother everyone was there. So, lot of people to take care of me and my child along with my husband.

At around 2:15 PM in afternoon, the doctor took out my child through C section and as soon as he was out, he started crying so loudly, that whole floor said this boy is crying like a 6-month-old. He is so clever. I was so happy when I heard him crying. I felt as if now I can sweetheart into my hands. And that feeling of parents are such that we can't express in words. That motherly bond gets started when the child is in womb. Every time during my last trimester whenever he was awake inside my womb and use to travel from here to there, I took the video of my stomach, felt like waves. So, at 2:15 pm doctor said to me "Congratulations, a healthy male child". For parents, it does not matter whether it's a boy or a girl child, what matters is a healthy baby. It's the society who are much interested in knowing the gender and sadly even if parents are very very happy with a girl child, still the society tries to poke their noses and try to console by saying, it's goddess Laxmi and I know if I would had a female child, everyone would have tried to pressurize me for another child hoping for a male child. Arjun's weight was around 3.6 kg and from Day 1, he started breast feed, nurses were surprised to see the way he was so much hungry, he knows how he will take his food. Also, since it was C section and unfortunately the bleeding was more, I had a blood transfusion that time and high fever and all these did not affect my happiness, I was very happy and within few hours the fever was also gone.

Since me and my elder sister who is my sister cum best friend, we both were pregnant during the same month. Her due date was just 15 days ahead of my due date. We decided two-two names each for boy and girl. So, we both decided Arjun name for my child and Avyan name for her child.

Arjun was born on 23rd April 2018 and Avyan was born just after 17 days on 10th May 2018. Since my symptoms or habits what we see in YouTube videos resembles as if baby girl will be born so, I purchased all the baby girl's cloths and till 2 months, I was making him look like a baby girl only. We moved to our new house on 20th April and 23rd April my son was born. He came to the new house on 26th April 2018. Things were going smoothly, we even passed the corona phases and all three of us me, my husband and son were enjoying, living peacefully. Everything was working good and we were having a happy life.

23-April 2023
His 5th B'day

Later, sometime around year 2021, we realized my son was different from others. He was not social with the children, don't like to play with toys, were more interested in numbers, like to be alone or with us only, only communicates with us and that too very little bit of communication as and when required and we were able to understood. But if any stranger also asks him math's table, within a second, he starts reciting. Academic wise he is brilliant but lacking in social interaction. This is why we took him to psychiatrist to know why he is so different from the other children. He was only asking us to buy those toys which has either number or alphabets written in it. He was not interested in remote cars or vehicle toys, train or soft toys. But when I purchased him a money bank toy, or a washing machine, or a fridge toy or an elevator he becomes happy and play with it continuously. Though now things have changed and he is liking carrom, ludo, ball, plays guitar, flute, sing songs and play with other toys as well, but before last year he was not interested at all. And he is so much interested in lift, that he can watch the lift entire day. He also likes to see how washing machine is rotating and all the electronics items.

Uncertainty: The Painful Experience

If you give him mobile, he can spend whole day watching lift, washing machine, numbers, table videos. We tried so many times that he also watches cartoons and learn from there, but he never watched.

Since his age was to play and mix up with children we took him to psychiatrist, then after few assessments she told us that he has the eye contact and the social smile but the number of words he should say was not up to the age and then some more assessment was done and then came to the conclusions that he is mild autistic. So, doctor advised speech and occupational therapy for him.

So, since he was not social, he did not like his fourth B'day as we invited a lot of people. Even when we celebrated his first B'day he did not like it and kept on crying, we thought due to hot weather he might be crying but then we got to know after seeing the crowd he becomes frustrated and he cries. But today he likes the crowd and enjoy every festival.

I felt so bad and guilty, as the person who should be the happiest on his birthday did not like the birthday celebration in society club.

So, in year 2023 he was having his 5th Birthday and it was an excitement for all three of us as we have planned to celebrate his birthday in Goa. Though summer is considered as an off season for Goa, but during summer the hotels are cheap and affordable and easily available. We both already applied our leaves 3 months back and from January we have started making plans and waiting early for the 23rd April.

First, we decided to go by flight as flights are mostly cheaper from Pune to Goa, but later on considering Arjun's excitement for train journey as kids these days like train journey more adventurous than flight journey.

When we were kid, we usually travel in trains or buses only, so flight was only a dream to us, but it was not affordable as the salaries were very less of our parents those days and only rich people used to travel by flights. And now people are so busy and occupied that mostly people choose flight over train as the flight take less time.

And the time came, we were at the Pune Railway station waiting for Goa express, Arjun was so much excited I cannot tell. The train got 2 hours late but still that excitement of boarding the train was there on my son's face. The train came and we boarded the train and took our seats, I also took his favorite toys, drawing copy, math's book in one bag and he was so excited that it was like a moving home to him, he was doing all those activities which he does in home. We tried to make him sleep in the train but he didn't as he thought if he sleeps, he will miss some of the train moments.

And finally at around 11 he slept and in the morning around 6 am we reached Goa.

When Madgoan station came he was very happy, all the time there was a smile on his face, every moment we were enjoying right from boarding. We mostly prefer to take hotels in south goa as the crowd is less and more peaceful than north goa. We booked a hotel, walking distance from Colva beach in a very reasonable price. In 2016 also when Arjun was not born, we went to goa in the same hotel and now in 2023 also we visited same hotel, but there was so much difference what it was earlier and what it is today, might be due to covid 19, the business got lost and so the hotel was not in good condition this time. One more reason to book this hotel was, we both (me and my husband) don't explore much, if we liked some places, we will keep on visiting same place until we get bored. same in case of songs also, until we get bored, we will listen same songs in a repetitive mode. Even if anyone ask about the hotel in Goa we refer the same hotel to them, maybe they don't like. When my sister and brother-in-law went to Goa, they also stayed in the same hotel.

Sometimes we think may be our repetitive behaviors is in our son gene also, he also is very repetitive and when I was a kid, I was not social at all. I don't know whether I was an introvert or what, but I fear going to school on an auto or bus where I have to face so many other children. I like going to school with my father only. In classroom also, even after knowing the answer I fear in raising my hands. Don't know whether the behavior was kind of introvert, shyness or self-mutism, those days we rarely listen these terms autism, self-mutism, psychiatrist, ADHD etc.

As soon as we reached Goa, we borrowed scotty on rent. Everything was full of excitement for us, going to hotel by scotty, I was carrying suitcase in my hand and Arjun was standing in front and my husband was driving. After reaching hotel, we got freshened up and without wasting any time directly went to beach. Also, we were fortunate enough that the weather was not that much hot what we expected. Arjun was so happy on the beach; he was enjoying every waves coming to him and happily going to the waves and then running back. It was so much fun. We also had a motor ride on the beach. The environment was so peaceful and calm, we were living every moment there. Seeing him enjoying on his birthday, made us to order a drink for us, as we were so much happy. We were feeling like a heaven and thinking life is so good, no work, no office, no one else, just relax in beach order the food and drink and enjoy.

We also made a friend from Bangalore, they visited or hotel room while we were celebrating Arjun's birthday.

While coming back to Pune, we thought since we had a very good trip, now we can focus on our office work and Arjun can focus on his studies and the activity classes.

Same time, our offices started in a hybrid model so need to go to offices at least 2 days a week. So, I called my parents for the help and to take care of Arjun.

We were also worried about Arjun's 5th year vaccination.

Things were going very good, we both started gym, Arjun started his guitar classes and summer camp. He started engaging with other children, made two friends also in his school. Slowly his speech also got improved and started making friends and playing with other children in summer camp. Life just came to track for us.

We were only worried about his 5th year vaccination and we got the appointment on 19th May 2023 in one Multispecialty Hospital (where Arjun was born) in Pune for his vaccination. The doctor gave the vaccine on his leg and he cried a lot in pain. After 2 years, he visited hospital, as he was so healthy not even have cough or fever in the past 2 years. In 2022, he was detected dengue, but just after few days he was absolutely fine and for that I want to thank my one of society friend who suggested me a technique to increase platelets. She told me just crush some raw papaya and carrot in daal and give him, his platelets will not come down due to dengue.

We never thought that after this, our whole life is going to take a U turn. Doctors already informed us that he might get fever after the vaccination and we were ready for it.

He did not get any fever till 4-5 days, but after few days suddenly he started lymping and was refusing to eat anything. He was having difficulty in swallowing food, just was interested in liquid diet, was not taking solid food at all, when we showed to pediatric doctor, they told everything looks fine in mouth, no mouth sores or ulcer is there.

And after few days, his mouth was okay and he was able to swallow (we still did not find the reason why he was unable to swallow), at least we got relaxed now. Then we went to the orthopedic doctor for lymping, he took out some X-rays and everything was normal, but lymping did not stopped. If he had fallen down, then if lymping was there, then we might have thought it's okay, but one night before his walking was okay and suddenly in the morning when he waked up, he was unable to walk properly. This left us in confusion that this is not correct, something is wrong. Our biggest pain as a parent was, we are the parents of a mild autistic child who have the capability to bear a pain but would not tell his parents or anyone. We always have to guess the pain he might be having and luckily our guesses are mostly correct. But same time we also think that, what if something happens to us, who is going to understand his pain and his feelings. 31st May 2023 was his last Guitar class of that session, we thought that once the school opens, he will not get the time to learn guitar. That day only Guitar teacher called us that Arjun have done potty in the gallery and in his pants. We were in shock, because he was 5 years old and he always did potty in commode only, he have the capability to hold the potty till he reaches home and at least he knows that he need to ask the teacher for going to potty. Somewhere we were thinking that all these symptoms are not good, it's a sign of weakness. When he was 3-year-old, he learned to do potty in commode or potty seat only nowhere else, but suddenly he did potty in his pants that means he was not okay.

We went quickly to teacher's home, washed her gallery and cleaned his clothes and then took him in my lap and loved him and kissed him to make him feel okay and not something which he did wrong. His eyes were also dull and was seeing very weak. But whenever we were taking him to doctor's they were just asking if he had fever, but since fever was not there so they were saying everything is okay. We were making him eat all the healthy foods so he can become healthy. Then on 5th June 2023, he caught fever, we went to doctor's clinic, he was the doctor from same multispecialty hospital where Arjun took his vaccination. He suggested some antibiotic tablets for 5 days and ordered few tests such as CBC (complete blood count) and CRP (C-reactive protein).

CBC was normal, but the CRP was very high. CRP or ESR tests mostly denotes the inflammation /infections in our bodies. Though these are medical terms, we are not doctors, but this is what we think and as per google. So, after taking five days medicine, Arjun was fit and started his daily activities, going to school, tuitions etc. lymping was also reduced, his food intake was also proper. But after a week only, he again caught fever. This seems very unusual to us, as till the antibiotic was given that time, he was fine, as soon it was stopped, he again caught fever.

This time we changed the doctor, went to other doctor who was from same multispecialty hospital. We refer these doctors as they know the full background of Arjun since birth and their medicines well suits Arjun.

This doctor is very good and much experienced than the previous doctor, we have full faith in him. His diagnosis is very good and quick. He ordered a covid antibodies test and CRP test. Those reports came the same day in evening and at night around 10:30 pm, the doctor called us in clinic. He told us to get him admitted as the covid antibodies report was positive. We asked the doctor, "When he would have caught covid as he did not have any kind of cough or fever". To this he replied few children had covid in year 2022 but there was no covid symptoms at all but the antibodies are already built up in them. If the antibodies are in normal range than that is okay, but higher range of antibodies needs to be treated. He suggested a five days course of medicine which will lower the high value of covid antibodies. We admitted him in the same hospital where few steroids was given to lower the antibodies. After that the COVID antibodies was normal, CRP was normal, mostly all the reports came normal and he was fine and playing. Doctor called us for a follow-up on 1st July 2023 after a CBC test.

Earlier we thought, now that he is fine, not lymping, eating properly, no fever, no infections, more active, no dullness, even if we skip the blood test or follow up then that would be fine. We thought of being careless, but suddenly don't know what happened to us, we discussed and agreed to let's go for CBC and a follow-up, if the doctor have suggested then it would be for our betterment only. So, Arjun had his CBC test and to our astonishment all the values were very very low. His hemoglobin was 6.5, platelets was 150000 (it's considered normal in few report) and white blood cell count was around 3.5. He compared these reports with the previous reports and told us all the values are decreased within 10 days only, so we must go for a bone marrow test. He explained us that we should always see the hemoglobin (HB), platelets and WBC if all three are in normal range or not, if all are either high or all are either low then we must go for a bone marrow test. Bone marrow is a soft tissue inside your bones that produces blood cells and platelets.

We usually only see Hb and platelets count whether normal or not, and skip WBC values. We should always monitor the WBC as this is the main parameter. If it's lower than normal range or higher than normal change we must consult a doctor.

I heard the bone marrow test when I was in class 6. We used to watch the daily soap "Kasauti Zindagi ki" and in that there was one character whose name was" Sneha" had to go through bone marrow transplant as she was having blood cancer. It just clicked my mind and I was very worried.

As the doctor came, I asked doctor why he suggested bone marrow test and just to make me calm he said very casually that it's just to know the infections and other things. But still I was not satisfied with his answer, somewhere the Kasauti Zindagi ki character was revolving in my mind and I was having very negative thoughts. I told my husband," I suspect cancer" he said you are overthinking, be calm it would be just an infection.

Bone marrow test happened in which there is a spring like injection which is drilled inside the bone marrow spine, it is mostly given under local anesthesia.

Arjun's BM Report

We saw the report and we were googling everything written on the report and our intuition says something is very serious which the doctors are not confirming.

We were asking all the doctors who were coming on round, but they were just saying when the senior doctor will come, he will inform us about the report. Then somewhere the next morning a one doctor came and told us that it's a leukemia so treatment will go on for this.

We searched what is leukemia and the answer was a type of blood cancer. We both started crying but still somewhere we had a hope that may be the senior doctor will say nothing serious just an infection or something. In the evening the senior doctor came and told us we need to admit Arjun in "Dinanath Mangeshkar hospital". He stated that going forward the treatment will continue from there. He told us same thing that he is having leukemia, a type of blood cancer.

As soon as we heard, we both were shocked and unstoppable tears started rolling down from our eyes. I was like what sins me or my family have done that a 5-year-old boy has to suffer so much. Even though I don't believe much in God or karma after I started following Osho principles. But still I prayed to take my life and give a long life to my son. I prayed God for his good health and same time I was cursing the God why it happened to us. And literally speaking earlier I still had some faith but after this incident I lost all the faith in god. I am now an atheist. I believe that if a superpower or a god is there, then he should have the ability to see who should be punished and who should not be punished, who is right and who is wrong. What kind of superpower or a god is!! that he can give so much pain to small children. At least if he has the super-power, he must be able to make sure that the children should not suffer. And if the super-power is there then he should make sure criminals should not be living a peaceful life. How is it possible that a rape happens in temples, mosques or churches and the god cannot do anything, let the people suffers. Whenever I look around, I see the helpful and true people suffers and the criminals, the liars don't suffer at all. They have a healthy and long living life. I stopped believing in Karma too, I have seen and felt if you do good to others, bad things will still happen to you. My boss was so good he supported me so much during my son's treatment but still he lost his one and only child in an accident. One of my dear friend who is so good and helpful lost her 2 year old child. So, I don't believe in God or karma now.

My 5-year-old boy was just in his development phase, just started making new friends, he just started some communication with his friends after the speech therapies. How can a god be so unfair that a child who is already mild autistic and undergoing speech therapy, started his good time suddenly suffers from this critical disease and have to undergo treatment. Initially we got his complaints from his school, but soon all the teachers started loving him as he is one of the brilliant boy in his school. Today he is 6-year-old and he knows the table from 1 to 40 and addition and subtraction of any big numbers which is mostly unbelievable when I tell anyone.

We were in tears, we did not had anything after hearing the words by doctor and we were hiding our tears from him as he was playing and absolutely fine at that time. Nobody can say he is having cancer after seeing him, he was so joyful, playing at that time. He was playing with chairs, remote, BP machine in the hospital and enjoying. Our mind was asking the same question" why him, why not us". The life would have been much better and we would have not faced such thing if we had no child. Somehow, we would have survived without having a child, but after giving birth to a child you get so much emotionally attached to him while he is in womb, then taking care of him, have made certain plans for him and suddenly when you hear that he is having a critical disease, how would you feel?!!

Two days our tears were uncontrollable and rolling from our eyes anytime.

My father came to the hospital with the food which my mom has prepared and he saw us crying, he was also shattered after hearing this and continuously consoling me that don't worry, everything will be alright, whatever treatment is needed we will do and he will live a long life. These consoling words somewhere relaxed us but we still know the truth is he is diagnosed with cancer.

Since cancer is a deadly disease, first I thought not to have any type of treatment as there is no guarantee of cure and my child is going to face the daily injections, chemotherapies etc. I know that since it's an acute blood cancer, the cells will still be there after the treatment so till the time he is with us, let's make him happy and do whatever he likes. I also made my plan that I will also take my life if something happens to him, because I cannot imagine my life without him, cannot spend a single moment without him. I am so attached that I don't want him to go to schools also, just want him to be with me.

My father and my husband then made me understand that the treatment is must because many times, even after having cancer, people do survive and have a long life. My father started citing examples of the celebrities like Yuvraj Singh, Anurag Basu, Manisha Koirala, Mahima Chowdhary, Imran Hashmi's son etc.

And one truth is that injections pain is still bearable, but pain of children where the cancer was spread in the whole body, that pain is not bearable at all. I have seen them crying like anything, since the cancer is spread in all over the body so the joint pain, unable to walk, mouth pain, hand pain, the pain spreads everywhere when the cancer spreads in body. Injection pain is still bearable by kids and also there is a positivity of progress with each injection, that it will surely going to kill cancer cells, but without treatment the condition of cancer patient become worse. So, we decided to let's start with the treatment without any further delays.

Finally, we called the doctor who did the bone- marrow, he was a very nice person and shared his personal number to us to guide us. He was having zero attitude.

We called him after getting discharged from hospital and asked him "which hospital we should prefer for the treatment". He told us that Tata memorial is the best hospital and we should not be going anywhere else. Arjun report says that the cancer cells i.e., blasts are 20 percent, a normal healthy human may have 5 percent blasts of cells. If it's more than 5 percent it's needs to be treated. He told us that since it's 20 percent, you can start the treatment from tata hospital without wasting any of the time.

Feelings And Emotions

So, we came back from hospital after we got to know about Arjun is having leukemia. We all discussed and decided for the further treatment in Tata Memorial Hospital (TMH).

I have my best friend living in the same society and same building. She is my best friend from my engineering days from first semester and we are still maintaining the same friendship till today. When you have a friend near you, you can never be depressed, whenever I feel low, I go to her home or call her and share her my feelings.

Firstly, I thought not to inform anyone, but you cannot hide anything from your best friend. As soon as she came to my home for asking Arjun's health I started crying and informed her, we both cried and cried and then she promised me she is not going to inform anyone about it and she really maintained that promise. I know she is very loyal friend to me.

Actually, I thought of not to inform anyone else, because if you see, till today people are mostly unaware of the diseases. They are unaware that cancer is not infectious. It is the cancer patient who should be more protected from other people so that he should not get any infections as a cancer patient immunity is already compromised.

If anyone asks us, we just say that since Arjun is having severe infections, so doctor have advised not to send him anywhere in crowd for at least 3 months. We informed people that we came to our hometown.

But people were so eager to see us, that once the three months passed, they again started asking me "Where are you", "When are you going to come back"," what had happened to you"," Is Everything all right"? May be the questions can be out of curiosity or maybe it can be a genuine concern, but I am aware that very few people have the genuine concerns, mostly people are curious to know about you.

Actually, I am an introvert and this could be the reason my son is also not social, even today he is not that social to play with the group of children. Since Arjun is not social so in order to make him social, I started becoming social, because kids mostly learn from their parents.

I was not at all interested in dancing but still I joined dance/Zumba classes, so Arjun also can learn from me and he can also dance. It's not like, I was not interested but I have a lot of fear inside me in dancing, singing or speaking in front of the crowd or even 3-4 groups of people. I even joined few ladies WhatsApp groups and also attended all the society functions just to be social. Frankly speaking now, I started enjoying in ladies' group, never felt ignored also by anyone. Earlier during my school and college days I mostly kept myself alone or with just one or two friend. I always thought my company is very boring to others. Whenever there was any school or college functions, I prefer to be absent because that fear of communication was always there. Going regular classes was altogether a routine, so there I didn't had a fear.

So tried myself to change so my son also get change and he will become social. And it really worked because earlier he behaves mischievously rather weirdly, starts crying anytime or do something that we don't go to the public places. But in malls, he enjoys, birthday parties he never enjoys, might be due to fear of balloon. He is very much afraid of balloon till today. In 2022, he started to enjoy Ganesh Chaturthi, Navratri, all the festivals he was enjoying. We were so happy to see the changes in him and even I was completely changed.

Earlier I thought, nobody should know about my son's disease, but somewhere I also want to show the world how strong we and our son is and not only this, I also wanted to let everyone be aware of the symptoms and the disease and take proactive measures if they see any such symptoms in any of their close one's ore relatives. I want my son to grow up, be a cancer survivor and read this book, have that confidence in him that he can tackle any difficult circumstances.

If he can sustain such hard circumstances, so whatever life brings him, any type of challenges, he can face without wrinkle on his forehead. I want to let him know that whether anyone is there with him or not, he is a one-man army, not everyone is as strong as he is.

Our Visit To Dadar

So finally, we decided we would not go anywhere else, but would take the treatment from Tata Memorial hospital, Parel, Mumbai.

We were so fortunate that during this crucial phase of diagnosis, my parents were there. They were taking care of me, my husband and my son. Sometimes, I still think what would have happened to us, if they were not with us during that time.

5th July 2023, we visited Tata memorial hospital, Parel. We were still not in a situation to eat anything. We did not had anything during our way to Mumbai also. We were just holding our tears. Anytime, tears were rolling down from our eyes and my mummy papa watching us in the mirror from the backseat of car. Every time, they were consoling us "Everything will be alright, don't cry", "Arjun will be alright and he is going to have a long life". And this is what is needed in that difficult situation, an emotional and mental support which makes you positive and optimistic.

Earlier, every 6-4 months, we make a trip to Lonavala, our friends always tease us like" why don't you buy your own farmhouse in Lonavala", "the way you guys visit there, it's like there should be a house of yours in Lonavala". And due to regular trip to Lonavala, Arjun was familiar with the road routes.

Uncertainty: The Painful Experience

Sad thing was Arjun was thinking we were going to Lonavala since Nani and nana (my parents) have visited Pune, so we are taking them to Lonavala trip. He was enjoying the trip as he was in hospital since 10 days, so he was thinking that we are taking him to trip. He was very very happy and excited, he also didn't have fever, no lymping, no health issues and absolutely fine and active. But since as per the reports there are 27 % cancer cells found in his blood which needs to be treated. He was so excited; he was playing the songs in full volume.

Now when you are in such a saddened situation and during that time whichever songs are being played or you have heard, will become very depressing songs for you as you are creating some bad memories with those songs and in future you will never want to listen those songs. If you listen again things get fall in place which you don't want to remember.

You will again feel those bad moments because those songs remind you of the bad days. These songs will keep on reminding me the bad days of your life.

And earlier we were loving those songs but then when it was being played in the car during our way to Mumbai, it was like all songs relatable for that situation which made us cry more after relating it to our life with those songs. Some of these songs were: "Main tere Ankho me Udasi", "Jihale Miskin", "Tum kya mile". Earlier we listen these songs in repeat mode but now we removed it from our playlist and if anytime comes on radio also, we skip it or turn off the radio.

So, finally after 4 hours of journey, we reached TMH, Parel and we did not get the parking in TMH. We were worried where to park the car now, we did not get any parking space in Dadar, and Dadar being the crowded city, we were forgetting our path and returning to the same location again and again.

So, we thought, first of all, let's find a hotel/lounge where there is a parking space and we can keep our bags in hotel and can park our car there. Since hospital allow only one attendant if the patient is an adult and for kids' patient, they allow mother and father both, so we were thinking at least if we get the hotel, my parents will stay there and then we can come to hospital for registration. We called almost 10 nearby hotels and none of them have parking area. Finally, we connected "Sharda Hotel" located near Kohinoor building, Dadar where the receptionist said don't worry, we will arrange some parking space for you. We saw in old Mumbai, there is no space for parking and people are parking their vehicles in the roadside only.

The hotel room was around 8*8 ft. with a small bathroom and we were five people, my mother, my father, my husband, Arjun and myself. Since it was in main Dadar, the cost was 3500/day without AC, and it was considered as cheapest as it was located in main Dadar and I know Dadar cost of living is very very high as compared to Navi Mumbai. I was living in Dadar only during my first job at Chinchpokli so I was aware of the cost.

My parents took in charge of all the other things, whether it's booking the hotel or arrangement of food as our whole day was being spent in hospital only. So, they only decided to take one room only as we don't know how much expenses we need in this treatment so why to waste money unnecessarily by taking two rooms as we were not there to spend holidays, we were there to successfully have the treatment in Tata Memorial hospital.

So, readers, you can't even imagine, how we all managed to stay in an 8*8 room and it did not even bothered to us as all we were thinking were about the successful treatment. But at the same time, now if I think about that situation, I just wants to salute my parents for the adjustments they did. In a small room, we three me my husband and my son was sleeping on the bed, and my parents were sleeping on the little space on the floor, just from one side, don't have space to turn from one side to the other.

Day 1 To Day 13 In TMH

After keeping our stuffs, we left the hotel and took a taxi to Tata Memorial Hospital. First day of the hospital was very hectic, we travelled from Pune to Mumbai, have not slept from 3-4 days neither had any food other than tea, then searched for the hotel, then came to TMH, where now we need to do the registration.

We went to the private registration bay, as we thought in private registration, the treatment will be more smooth as compared to General registration, but after reaching there the registrar told us that for children OPD's/doctors all are same in private as well as general, so better to go with General treatment rather than Private as there would be a huge amount of money which get spent in private treatment. OPD's, beds availability all are based either on the first come and first serve basis, or the age group or the criticality. We got to know that private registration is 4 times more than the general registration, so suppose if the treatment cost in general category is 1 lakh so with the same facility in private it would cost at least 4 lakhs. Private categorization is only beneficial in the case of adult patient. So, we went ahead with general registration.

After registration, we got a TMH card, just like our debit cards in which we need to recharge amount and for every billing it will be automatically deducted from the card. During registration, they ask our salary so if our salary is less or not earning the recharge is done by social worker and the treatment is done free of cost. But since we both were working, we told them the same and we only have to bear the cost and also our company insurance is there so most expenses gets claimed.

Now it was the time to visit the pediatric OPD. We got the appointment /token number as 101, so after 100 patients OPD's is done, then our number came. We waited for almost 4 to 5 hours and then our number came.

After visiting TMH, when we saw the crowd everywhere, we got to know how many people are struggling with this disease. All having a hope of life of their loved ones. And after visiting pediatric area we got to know so many children in India are suffering from blood cancer. We talk so much about Gen AI, cloud, latest technologies, but don't know why we are lacking in medical science.

The OPD was basically like a conference room where at least 10 doctors were sitting. Each doctor assigned with a patient. We were sent to a doctor whose name was also same as my son's name. He listened carefully, the whole story on how it started from the day of vaccination till the bone-marrow test. He advised some tests and then told us, that we need to come once we get the reports on our registered WhatsApp number and then meet the pediatric doctor.

Here only I also want to mention that when I asked doctor that "could this be due to vaccination"? he said it's nothing to do with vaccination. So at least our one confusion was clarified.

Since it was the first day and lot of communication happened with doctor, we didn't heard that we need to go to hospital once the report comes. We thought we need to go to doctor the next day to show the report as the OPD timing is 9 am to 5 pm and it was already 5 pm at the time of blood sample collection.

Somewhere around 8:00 pm, the reports came, but we did not visited the hospital as we thought the doctors might not be available at that time.

At night around 2:30 am, we got the call from doctor and she said in very angry tone, "why you did not come after the reports came, the report shows the potassium is high and we need to give him nebulizer immediately".

In response, we said that we are on the way coming to hospital, and we thought the doctors won't be available now. To this she told us that in tata hospital the doctors will be available 24*7, so don't assume doctors are not there.

That day, we got the scolding with the doctor and she was angry during the call, but was very sweet as a person. And frankly saying, her scolding made us feel that we are at the correct place for the treatment. We realized that my son's treatment is in right hand as this is the best hospital. They are so much concerned about each patient. Their records are so up to date that even if we missed, they are surely going to remind and you will get a call.

Immediately we rushed to hospital at 2:30 AM for giving him nebulizer.

Same day on 6th July 2023, we again visited the OPD's where the reports were reviewed again by the doctor.

Again, our OPD's turn came late as since morning 3 am we were in hospital and got free at 9 am in the morning after giving him Nebulizer and lowering his potassium level.

Then we rushed to hotel, gave him food as he did not had anything since night and woke up at 3 am only. And again, rushed to hospital, our each and every minute was so expensive and busy. I have not seen my phone since I reached Mumbai.

Finally, around 4 pm our turn came and same doctor was assigned to us, he told us "Tomorrow i.e., 7th July 2023 there would be a bone marrow test so don't make him eat anything after 12 pm at night and don't give any liquid after 7 am, as the bone marrow will be done at 9:30 am morning".

I asked doctor why again the bone-marrow test as it already done before coming to TMH.

He said there can be difference in values so we mainly trust the one which is done in TMH.

So, 5th and 6th July 2023, we spent almost entire day and night in hospital. 7th July 2023 morning was the bone marrow test and one of the best things about the hospital is, their first priority is always children. They gave us the bone marrow test timing as 9:30 am and exactly at 9:30 only, they started the bone marrow test. Doctors, nurses and all the staffs are very punctual with the timings unlike doctors, staffs I have seen in private hospitals. In private hospitals, I have only seen the management, housekeeping are punctual but not the main staffs. And in Tata, they will not admit the person unnecessarily unlike few private hospitals where it is most like a business, they admit the patient for making more money out of it. So, if there is no admit, the patients are more comfortable and have that mindset that there is nothing to worry, they will not get into depression and afraid about it.

If you get admit you will feel more like a patient. I like this in TMH. It's not like they will not admit at all, if they think that some cases need to be admitted they are going to take proper care of it, but for regular Bone marrow test and other things they will not admit. When we were in Pune and had bone marrow test in Multispecialty hospital, they admit Arjun for one day and he got very frustrated in hospital.

After the Bone marrow test, we visited OPD, the doctor asked us "where are you staying as of now", we said in hotel, so he told us to start searching for the flat in Mumbai because during treatment we have to stay nearby only. He also asked us to visit social worker to get the expense for treatment and funds. And told us the bone marrow report will come on 11 so the next OPD will be only after the report comes.

We were not sure what is social worker for, when we visited, we got to know that most children are getting the treatment free of cost. Since we both are working parents, we refused for any funds, we told them as of now we don't require and our companies have 8 lakh insurance coverage for us. Still the social worker told us that in future if you require any funds or there is any need of large amount of money, we can still reach out to them for funds.

In TMH, most of the treatment is being done with the help of funds only. Almost 90 percentof the pediatric patient treatment is done free of cost, we were paying because we already have the coverage in our company. And I really admire the hospitality they have for children, the support which Tata hospital gives. Even a poor can take the best treatment in tata hospital without having money. Not only treatment but they have certain hostels also with very less price, where parents can live with children during the treatment.

On 8th July 2023, we came back to Pune, we did packing as now we have to shift to Mumbai for at least a year and leave Pune Everyone in our families were worried, they keep on calling us and telling us if you need anything just give us a call. My sisters and brother calling me back-to-back "Don't worry be calm and we are just a call away", "anything needed please don't hesitate, we will do whatever is needed and Arjun will be alright, no need to worry". My brother usually don't call, but that time every hour he was calling and sending money even when I was telling him it is not required as of now. He was saying" We will do everything for Arjun and no need to worry, he will be fine in just few days you will see". My elder sister who is a teacher in a private school told me "I have some savings, let me know if you need for treatment". I feel blessed to have such family. If you are around positive people, you will surely get the strength and I got this strength as my family was my backbone and that's the time, I realized why family support is important.

When we reached Pune, my brother informed us that, there is a TMH center in Kharghar, Navi Mumbai also, he got to know from his friend. Since we were not sure whether it's an operational center or it's a kind of institution only where doctor's nurses might be getting training and all, we were in little confusion whether to go to Navi Mumbai or be in Parel only.

Later on, after exploring out more we got to know that it's operational and newly opened branch and is less crowded than TMH, Parel. And everything is same as TMH, Parel, same pediatric doctors report here also.

The three days in Pune 8th, 9th, 10th we were packing our bags, sometimes crying too, what life have given to us.

How can someone be so unlucky like us! And I just made my mind, that whatever my son wants in life I will do everything for him, whether it's good or bad! Since he is mild autistic, he loves lift, I thought I am going to buy lift toys for him, I will install lift at my village, so wherever he goes, there should be a lift. He will have his own lift and can press button as many times as he wants.

On 11th we again went back to TMH Parel from Pune as the registration was done in TMH Parel only, so for taking the treatment in TMH Kharghar branch, there would be some formalities to be done.

Again, we visited the same hotel in Dadar, kept our luggage in hotel. Now the receptionist was so friendly that he asked us to stay in AC room in a price of a NON-AC room. I have seen Mumbai people are very very helpful in every terms.

Whenever my mother was alone in the room and we were in hospital, they keep on coming and asking my mom "Auntie if you need anything, please let us know".

When we visited TMH Parel OPD, somehow our number came within an hour only, we informed the doctor that we want to continue the further treatment in TMH Kharghar branch i.e., ACTREC.

The doctor confirmed us whether we have any flat or apartment or relatives in Kharghar, we lied them and said yes.

For doctors, the first thing they want is before starting the treatment, the patient should have a comfortable flat to live and the flat should be nearby the hospital so if any emergency comes, the patient should reach hospital in 10-15 minutes.

So, the doctor called the doctor in ACTREC branch and told her about Arun's case id and to transfer the file to ACTREC branch. She mentioned in the file that the treatment will be continued from Kharghar branch and mentioned the pediatric oncologist whom we need to meet on 13th July 2023 in Kharghar. Same day she also advised few steroids tablets which Arjun have to continue from 13th July. So basically, the treatment got started from 13th July where it started with steroids tablets. The doctor also attached the protocol of first phase of treatment which is called the "Induction Phase".

On 13th July, we have to visit the Kharghar branch, till now i.e., 12th July we were in Sharda hotel in Dadar only. We were continuously searching for the flats through various websites, but did not get any flats in Kharghar or nearby location. Whatever number we were calling were that of broker and their charges was very very high.

And same day I got a call from my brother's friend, we call him Suraj (name changed) Bhaiya. He told us meanwhile please come to my place, then we will together search for an affordable flat for us which should be nearby to the hospital. Without wasting a single minute, we checked out the hotel, went to his home as our OPD was next day.

And seriously, I have never seen such a family in my whole life, I never thought that somebody can be that much helpful and supportive. He is not in our blood relation then also he helped in our most difficult situation.

He gave us his entire 3 BHK flat along with 2 cooks and a maid and told us to only concentrate on treatment no need to worry about other things. He told us to live there comfortably till the time we can find a good flat near the hospital. Since he himself is a builder, so he was aware of where to find the flats whom to contact, which broker would be good to us to contact. He and his wife were living at the 6th floor and we were at 2nd floor. Both of them were very concerned about Arjun. They were having 3 flats in the same building.

We were so hungry when we reached there, as soon as we reached, we got freshened up, then cook served us meal, we ate and then relaxed little bit. Whenever my mom or myself was trying to do anything the maid and cook were like, "no ma'am we could not allow you to do any work, just we are here to follow the orders ", "just you have to order and we will do whatever you want". Even they did not allow us to buy any vegetables, they were like this is our work. Every time, they were like if you need anything just let us know.

Since we are from lower middle-class family, we never got treated like this before, sitting idle and everything coming to us.

His flat was in CBD Belapur, which was almost 30 min away from hospital.

We stayed there for almost 13 days, searching our flats also side by side. Our main focus area to search the flat was somewhere in Sector 30, 34 and Sector 35, as the hospital would be just 5 min away from there.

Finally, we found a flat in Sector 34, the rent was around 19K/month and it was a 2bhk unfurnished flat. We needed at least 2 room and a hall because my parents were also going to stay with us.

When we informed this to Bhaiya and his wife in who's flat we were staying, they told us please shift only when you find a good place otherwise stay here only.

I cannot forget them in my whole life, they supported us in a very crucial time.

So finally, all was set, the hospital was nearby, every basic facility nearby only and we also brought our scotty from Pune.

Whenever my husband or my father were visiting Pune for anything, my best friend was always ready with tea, lunch or snacks. Since she is my college time best friend, she is like a family to us.

Before I forget, I also want to mention here that my perception got changed completely for minorities. The flat which we got was surrounded by mostly minority community. Earlier I was little bit afraid/scared when I have to travel places where minorities are in more numbers, but now after living in this area I came to know they are very very good and helpful. They were ready to support us anytime we needed.

Whenever we were meeting them, they always greet us smiling and made us feel very comfortable. From a small kid to old people, everyone greeting and asking if you need any help just let us know.

They never made us feel we are from different religion and during Arjun's chemotherapy when Arjun hair fall started, they never made any surprise faces or shocking faces, always saying to us he will be alright soon.

I still have seen few people on street seeing him with full surprise making him feel uncomfortable. Though Arjun is autistic, but those days whenever he was looking into the mirror, he feels little sad and that's the reason to normalize his hair fall and his baldness, Arjun's father also clean shaved his head all the time. Whenever we were going to hospital sometimes people get confused as who is the patient, father or a child as both were bald.

Causes Of Ball
(B-Cell, Precursor Acute Lymphoblastic Leukemia)

During these times, whenever we were having our phones, every time we were checking/ googling what are the main causes/symptoms/ survival rates of BALL.

We have subscribed all the professors of medical colleges or institutions who give lectures on YouTube, we also subscribed every channel related to oncology, leukemia.

I remember, I was looking at one of the videos where one professor was explaining the difference between T-ALL cancer and B-ALL cancer and he also mentioned few causes of BALL, which I will try to describe below but since these terms are medical related, I also understood just little bit of it.

- **Genetic:**

Meaning hereditary, so if any of our ancestors or earlier generation have any type of blood cancer, so there are chances that any of the coming generation also can have it.

- **DNA Chromosomes Changes:**

Some genetic mutation changes or DNA chromosomes changes can also cause cancer such as IgH, IgG deletion, ETV-RUN X1 etc. I don't want to get into these details as all these are biological/medical terms and I don't have much idea on these. I am just mentioning here whichever information I got from YouTube videos.

- **Benzene chemical:**

Few chemicals such as benzene can also cause cancer which is found in detergent, pesticides, paints, burning tyre etc.

Now if we look at the first cause, the chances were less as both our parents (My mother, MIL, FIL and father) all are healthy and active till date. All of them have crossed 70 years and for all the CBC report are mostly good, only the disease they are having is either BP or Sugar which is quite normal.

Even me and my husband have regular checkups and reports are mostly fine.

It may happen that the generation before our grandmother or grandfather could have cancer but we are not aware of it.

Second cause was related with DNA changes so it's basically a medical term, so we were unable to relate.

Third cause was the valid cause for us to think upon. In Nov 2022, during Diwali, we painted our homes with luster paint, not only homes but me and Arjun also painted some flower pots in our balcony and even had pesticides control in our house. And we were there in the room while the work was going on. So, benzene chemical could be the reason for cancer.

Both me and my husband came to this conclusion that it could be due to benzene chemical which might have released during the painting of houses.

Both of us thought to ask this with the doctor, so during the next OPD, we asked these questions that is it possible that the reason of my child having cancer is benzene? To which, doctor said "Please don't worry, it is nothing like that, everything in google or YouTube is not correct. And we should try to accept the fact that your son is having leukemia which is curable once we take proper treatment and care and certainly, he will have a long life". He told us to move on with this fact which was very difficult for parents to accept.

After few days, we saw a baby of 3 months who was having leukemia. After seeing such a small baby, I was sure that there is no such cause, it can happen to anyone. If a breastfeed baby can have it, then anyone can have it.

First Phase Of B-ALL Treatment

My son was placed in a high risk of B-ALL protocols. This was because, he underwent few periods of steroids for 5 days, when we got him admitted the the multispecialty hospital initially. This was due to his COVID antibodies was high in number which has to be reduced, so doctor gave him 5 days steroids from 22nd June to 26th June 2023.This happened before the cancer was diagnosed. So, if any sort of steroids or some outside treatment is given to a pediatric patient, TATA team keep those patients under high risk because on the eight day of treatment some diagnosis is needed which cannot be done if there is any type of outside treatment or if any steroids were given previously. Due to this, they kept my son case under the high risk and I read somewhere that it's an assumption that the relapse rates are lesser in high-risk protocol than the standard/intermediate protocol as the chemotherapy given in high risk are more intense than the standard protocol or intermediate protocol but it's just an assumption that the relapse rates are less. Relapse depends on case-to-case basis. And of course, an oncologist will know more than us or google, because they are specialist in treating cancer, so their ultimate goal is how to cure a cancer patient and they do their best to make a patient recover.

So, on 13th July when we reached ACTREC, Kharghar for the first time, we were little relaxed as there was very less crowd as it was newly opened branch. Unlike TMH Parel, there was lot of parking area and much advanced technologies being used such as for Token number we don't have to make a queue and wait, instead just if we have the bill and there was a machine when we press it's buttoned the token number gets generated.

Doctors attached the high-risk Induction protocol for Arjun in the first phase of the treatment. It started with steroids for few days followed with some hard chemotherapies.

Induction phase chart was of 35 days and once the induction phase gets over again it will be followed by a bone marrow test to know how effective was the induction phase chemotherapy.

So, a third time, my son have the bone marrow test to check how much percentage of the cancer cells are remaining after the first phase of treatment.

Initially, my son's weight was 17 kg when the cancer was diagnosed, but after few days only, he put on 2 kg weight due to steroids. Steroids is a kind of medicine which will increase your weight, swelling happens and the people look fat, so those who don't know, will think that the child is becoming healthy but it's not like that. His body parts, hand and face got swollen and weight was increased to 19 kg. He was looking very different that time. We discussed the same with doctor that "why his cheek looks like swollen" to which doctor replied "It's expected because he is on steroids and in upcoming months, he will again become normal".

When you work in office, you have office friends, when you go to college, you will have college friends, same like that, we have made some very good friends there who were sailing in the same boat as us. They were also struggling with their kid's cancer treatment. We exchanged numbers and sometimes call each other and share our feelings, because we can only share our feeling with those who will understand our scenarios and can feel the same. Since all of us sailing in the same boat understand each other and give advice to each other, what to give the kids and what to avoid. I was the only working mother in that group and people tends to have the feeling that working mother will know much what to give, what not to give. They think that since she is working on laptop so she is more educated. :D

I want to mention about my friends here in my book, one was from Arunachal Pradesh, one was from Gaya, Bihar.

So, while talking to other parents, we got to know that while having the cancer treatment, kids mostly refuse to take meals or even if they take it would be a very very less meal. And this is due to the high doses of chemotherapy.

For few of the children, if the BMI index (Body Mass Index) come at a low level, children who are refusing to eat had to insert a nutrition pipe in the nose. These kinds of situations scared us a lot when we imagine, because, Arjun is very very different from other children. He will certainly harm himself and remove the pipe if gets inserted in his nose.

We started thinking what if Arjun stopped eating, how we are going to convince him to have a nutrition pipe inserted in his nose.

And to our astonishment, the case turned entirely different for Arjun, he started eating more than his usual diet. Every two hours he gets hungry and we were like what to cook now? Not only hungry but every time he gets hungry, he becomes angry, cries and too much mood swings. But at least we were happy by heart that he is eating and then thought that might be the case is different for each child.

But later after some more discussion and OPD's, that the child eats more in induction phase due to the intake of steroids tablets. Steroid can make a person feel more and more hungry and every two hours, the patient will be a urge to eat something and so was the case for Arjun. Same experience was for almost all the parents. Later we came to know that the children don't eat at the time of second phase of treatment.

I can still remember my mother was putting beetroot, papaya and raw banana in almost every other food item which she cooked. Sometime she makes beetroot paratha, sometime palak paratha and if he is not eating that way then in pulse only, she was mixing all the healthy vegetables. Beetroot helps in improving the hemoglobin level and papaya is very good source for increasing the platelets count. So, we were like his counts should not drop, whatever healthy cells are suppressing by chemotherapy should get automatically recovered without any platelets or blood transfusion. We thought like this way. One thing we should always follow is taking a balanced diet, every nutrient is important, whether it's carbohydrates, protein, zinc, vitamins etc.

Chemotherapy drugs not only kills the cancer cells but also the healthy cells, so if a diet is proper the recovery of the healthy cells is fast.

In TMH and ACTREC Kharghar, there were not only the oncologist OPD's but also a regular follow-up needs to be done with infection control department and with Dietician, because in chemotherapy, the immunity goes down so the infection control department made the people aware how to avoid the infections. They gave us a solution which we need to dilute in warm water and Arjun have to daily sit in that diluted warm water in order to avoid infection. And mouth sores chances also get increases due to low immunity so they gave mouth paint, some mouth gel and mouth wash to daily clean Arjun mouth in order to avoid mouth infections. We need to visit them on regular basis and if any day we missed then they are surely going to shout like" what kind of parent you are, why you guys are not serious". Till now we did not get any shouting as we were regularly visiting but we heard these sentences from few people.

Dietician suggested us to include nuts and protein a lot in the diet during chemotherapy which we can get through dry fruits and food such as our Indian daal rice. She told us to add most pulses and vegetables in his diet. She also suggested to peel the fruits or vegetables in such a way that the peeling should remove a thick outer layer of the fruits or vegetables and after peeling we have to wash them in warm water. This is because now a days there are chemical substances over the fruits and vegetables so peeling off thickly and washing with warm water will help to remove the chemical substances. Till date we are following the same method for a speedy recovery.

That time my son "Arjun" was the most famous child of tata hospital Kharghar. The reason was he not only cry loudly but keep on saying loudly "sister -brother go from here" and all the sister brothers are like" okay we will go but are you going to do our work" :D. Every day same conversation happens between nurses and Arjun. He was famous because, the sisters and brothers were like" Oh my god, Arjun came". Now along with us, they were also worried how to put cannula or do blood test of Arjun. For other children it was much easier though the children cries a lot but they don't shake their hands as Arjun used to shake his hands. Firstly, when we tell the nurses that it's a difficult task to put cannula in Arjun hands, they are like it's okay we handle most children, but later on once they interacted with Arjun, then they came to know that what we were saying is correct. Actually, in Arjun's case, Arjun cry a lot and he shake his hand in such a way that the nerves which are visible suddenly get lost. So, nurses always say only Arjun is the boy whose nerves are so good that in only one prick, the blood can be taken out, but don't know how he shake his hand from internal that those nerves get lost suddenly. This makes him different from other children as other children do cry but it is easier for nurses to prick them as they don't shake their hands in this way. Since Arjun is autistic also so he doesn't think about his pain. He never understands that if he does that way, there would be more pricks for him. He thinks that if he does that way he will win. So, it's little hard for nurses to handle him.

As soon as he enters the ward, all nurses are like, "seems like Arjun came, who is going to prick him today", they discuss each other. And some sisters are like, let me handle him today, they come with so much confidence as if they will get promoted after successful putting cannula in Arjun's hand and then he/she is going to call 5 6 nurses to hold him because not possible single handedly handling him.

Through this medium of my writing this experience I would like to thank all brothers and sisters of Tata hospital for handling my son so politely and treated him so well. Arjun, my son is very very good and disciplined child, but being mild autistic, he doesn't understand what is the pain he has to go through, what things will hurt him.

At least minimum of 7-8 nurses were required for him to insert cannula in his veins. An autistic child may look weak, but he has more internal power as compared to other children. So, as I already mentioned, even when his nerves were visible, he used to shake his hands in such a way that the brothers and sisters get confused and would not able to find that nerve which they just saw. Though they find hard to manage Arjun, but whenever Arjun was coming, they have a big smile on their face.

At the starting they thought that he is like other children so if they shout on him, he will be afraid or will be quiet, but the situation was different for Arjun, once he gets familiar with anyone, then only he is going to allow you to shout on him or love him, otherwise you cannot shout on him, if you shout, he will cry in a more louder voice. Initially they felt irritated, but later on they started loving him more than any other children. They talked about Arjun only with each other. Sometimes even when we don't recognize them, they are like I know you are Arjun's parent. He has become this much famous there.

Days passed and after few days, whenever we were visiting in the ward, the brother and sister were like, let me handle Arjun today. It was like a competition for them that whom Arjun is going to like, deserve to be the best nurse.

Regular insertion of cannula/blood test became a part of life for us and Arjun.

Me and my husband also regularly calls pathologist for our blood test so that Arjun don't feel that he is alone getting those injections/pricks, everyone have to go through so even my Mumma and papa also getting injections.

Days were passing and soon came the 30th day of the induction phase, as I told earlier that the induction phase consists of 35 days. So, on day 30th, we were very worried as Arjun was suffering from cold and cough. We would not have worried this much if he was a normal child, since he was having cancer so cough and cold also worries us. Having cold or cough during the chemotherapy treatment is a sign of infections. For a cancer patient, the immunity is already compromised due to chemotherapy, so even a little issue worries us. And during those days, there were many pediatric patients with pneumonia cases, and out of this fear, the doctor asked us to admit him.

He went through few tests such as CRP which is done to check the inflammation, blood culture to test if any bacteria are present inside blood and CBC is done to check the regular counts.

Whenever I am mentioning blood counts, it means Hemoglobin, platelets, WBC counts and ANC (Absolute Neutrophils counts).

Till now, there was no admission in the hospital, he was just going to hospital and then coming back to home like an outpatient treatment. But now, the doctor asked us to admit him.

As I said, for Arjun being the mild autistic child, it was really tough to make him sleep in hospital. He can be in hospital during the day, but at night he will need his own bed, otherwise he will be awake entire night.

Two days we were in hospital, and both the days he cried so much for being in a hospital. Everyone trying to calm him down, but still he was crying a lot. One of the nurses tried to calm him down by scolding him, and this made us little angry so we asked her not to shout on him.

We try not to shout on him or scold him and so if anyone else shouts on him, we cannot tolerate. May be this behavior of ours is not justificable, but we know that an autistic child will never listen to you if you shout. If you shout then they will behave more mischievously. They will only listen if you show them calm behavior and love.

In TMH or ACTREC, all nurses including all sisters and brothers are well trained and their behavior also are very good with children, but sometimes they are strict when the children are not listening at all. And they have so much patience level and understanding towards children, I just want to salute all of them. They are doing the most difficult job which go unnoticed.

Doctors suggest the medicine and write on the file, but ultimately the chemotherapy is given by nurses only. I must say and want to thanks them, the way they are handling so many patients daily with so much patience and care is an unbelievable task. The adult patient sometimes shouts also on the nurses, because cancer will make a patient stressful, but the nurses understand and never respond back and always have smile on their face.

So, three days passed in hospital somehow and all the tests were normal meaning he was just having a viral infection due to which fever came. Doctor told us not to worry and same day he gave us discharge summary. And the moment, the cannula was removed, the happiness was all over his face that now I am going back to my home from hospital. He was running here and there, teasing sister and all sisters and brothers were like," See Arjun now, he is not the same Arjun who was 3 days back crying continuously".

During those three days, since sisters and brother got to know about Arjun, they were coming to us when he was asleep and in a very very low voice, they were talking to us, because when Arjun was awake, he just starts shouting repeatedly and keep on saying "Brother, sister go from here" and starts crying.

The nurses explained us how to check the vitals and all, so we can do it ourselves without disturbing Arjun.

Arjun is always fine, if his parents doing anything with him, I know he is not going to cry if we insert cannula in his hands. His much concern is only a familiar person can touch him, insert cannula or check vitals, No one else should touch him. Sometime, when we look back, we are thankful that he was not social because the disease which he is having have to undergo 9 months to one year of treatment, and if he was social, he would have asked us why I am not going to school, where are my friends and all. As he is not social at all, he doesn't miss his any fellow, classmates or friends. He didn't miss his schools. He was attached to his teachers so he missed them little bit.

And since he was not social at all and don't like playing with a group of children, his chances of infection were also less.

Since when Arjun was 6 months old, I am playing with him. I always sit and play with him. Actually, I was unaware that this might cause him social issue. Since he got a friend to play with, he never got social with other children as his mother was always with him to play with. And always he wanted me only to play with him. Even today we both only play with each other, even while having a walk we both company each other. Sometimes few people see with a weird face as he is almost 6 and half years old and walking with his mother holding my hand children with age of 4 to 6 years, now prefer to play with other children instead of their mom dad. Sometimes people advise me also to let him play alone and if you are every time with him, he will not learn to be social and when children are with children, they learn a lot. But people don't know that situation is very different for Arjun because leaving him playing alone or with other kids is quite risky at this moment which we are going through.

Now we both, me and my husband, just try to make him happy in whatever way we can, in whichever thinks we need to get involve. I feel very bad when I have some office meetings or calls and he is feeling alone and getting bored.

One of his favorite things is elevator and lift, so I have promised him, when I will earn more money, I will surely be going to buy a duplex flat and there I will install a lift from ground to first floor.

Last Day Of Induction Phase

Finally, the 35th Day means the last day of induction phase treatment came. It was on 18th Aug 2023; he has to undergo a bone marrow test and the bone marrow test report would have to come after 3 days of the test.

This bone marrow test would show how much chemotherapy have worked; how many blasts cells are left in bone marrow after the first phase of treatment.

Our whole family were praying a lot during those days for the report to come as negative. My parents went to Siddhivinayak Mandir in Dadar, same day my in laws also arranged some pujas at home.

We were eagerly waiting for the report, again and again logging on the TMH portal to check if the report is negative or not. It was on 21st Aug 2023, I opened the TMH patient portal with a finger crossed and saw the provisional report already came. I downloaded it and then opened it. Due to internet issue, it was downloading very slowly and our heartbeat was very very fast due to anxiousness.

Finally, it got downloaded. The report says 3 % blasts, meaning the cancer cells are there. Again, we were worried as we thought that it should have come 0. Later on, we came to know that 5% cancer cells can be there in a healthy person also. But we were also worried that nowhere in report was mentioned anything about MRD (Minimal Residual Disease). MRD report determines the small number of cancer cells that remain in your body after cancer treatment is complete. MRD shows the number of cells remaining which cannot be seen through microscope also.

Sometimes even if the blasts come as below 5% but still MRD could be positive, meaning the cells can be clearly seen through microscope.

If the MRD don't come negative in the first phase of treatment i.e., the induction phase, so again a bone marrow test will be done after the second phase of treatment i.e., the consolidation phase.

For some pediatric patients, if after the first phase of treatment, the MRD report is positive, then there are most chances that it will comes negative after the second phase of treatment.

Only in some rare cases, if the MRD is positive after the second phase of treatment also, a bone marrow transplant is needed whose cost is around 20-40 lakhs.

In the provisional report we were only able to see the blasts percentage, so we were eagerly waiting for MRD report. After few days, when the final report got committed, it showed us the details of MRD also. The MRD value was 0.002 % of the cancer cells remaining, meaning that the MRD report was negative.

That was the day, our joy was having no bound at all, we were very very happy. It was one of the happiest moments during that time for us. Once we got to know the report was negative and as soon as I informed my mummy-papa, they were also very very happy, started thanking God.

That day my mom cooked poori, sabji, kheer and what not! whatever Arjun likes.

They started calling all of my family members to inform them about the report. Also offered prayer in the evening. Every time, they were thanking God, soon they also planned to again visit Siddhivinayak Temple to thank God for the good report.

And as I already told I am an atheist, not only because my kid is suffering, but also, I never have any worship kind of feeling, or never felt that any god is there. Since when I was small, I was told to offer prayer, as a daily routine only I offer prayer, but always was an atheist from heart. Though I follow my Hindu culture/traditions, but I am not a theist. I just follow because we are following since birth. And you have to follow your culture/tradition otherwise this society will never be going to accept you as an atheist. I am a follower of Rajneesh Osho. I also have studied few versus of Gita book and I am influenced by it. I also follow Dr. Vikas Divyakirti and Saurabh Dwivedi from Lallantop and I always want to listen these people. Listening and following these people makes me a strong atheist. I have also read "Bhagat Singh's Why Am I an Atheist", and feel like whatever he said in his book is so true.

May be a day will come, my son gets 100% cured, some miracle happens, then I will also start believing in some supernatural power.

I think that if a god exists so how he can see children with so much pain, so many cruel people are walking freely, nothing is happening to them and these small children are having disease like cancer. So many poor and needy people are there who sleep on road have nothing to eat, why God have not done anything to save them and why he have not make them rich or at least give them the basic necessity of living a life.

In my case, I think how can a god threatens a life of a small child who was first struggling with speech and autism, but as soon as everything was on track for him, God gave him such a deadly disease as cancer.

But still, when I heard my child MRD report is negative, I thanked God. Though as per me God doesn't exists, but still since childhood we are told to thank God and due to which after every successful work, we are thanking him.

Though it's being said that the blood cancer of children (pediatric BALL) is curable, but still, I don't have that faith that it's 100 percent curable.

Cancer is a disease where nobody is said to be 100 percent cured because the cancer relapses are high in number. Till today, we have not made so much advancement in medical science. We have made much advancement in technology such as Gen AI, cloud computing etc. but I still believe that we are still lacking in the advancement towards medical science.

I don't think, till now there is any such medicine for cancer by which we can conclude that now a patient is cancer free. I know CAR-T cell therapy is there, but this also cannot guarantee a 100% cure for cancer.

B-All Consolidation Phase High Risk

As soon as the Induction phase was completed and his MRD came as negative we thought that now might be there would not be any further treatment as the MRD is already negative. So happily, we went to the doctor during our OPD, and then she attached a high-risk consolidation phase chart. Then we came to know that even if the MRD is negative but the whole treatment phases we need to complete otherwise again the cancer cells will come back.

We again asked doctor why my son is still kept under high-risk protocol if his MRD has come negative. Replying to us, doctor said, "Once a treatment protocol started with high risk will continue to be the high-risk protocol till the end of treatment and good thing about the high-risk protocol is since in high risk the chemotherapy is intense and doses are high, so the relapse rates are low as compared to intermediate or standard risk."

One more thing, I would like to add here is relapses of cancer can happen anytime, the cancer treatment doesn't guarantee that now a person is cancer free. But at the same time, I read somewhere that taking a healthy and balanced diet, avoiding any type of outside or junk food, even the juice also should be homemade from juicer can be a preventive measure for relapses. And what I got to know from dietician that we should always prefer fruits than juice as juice doesn't contain fiber whereas a whole fruit does contain fiber.

And if a patient is capable of tolerating high doses of chemotherapy will have a less chances of relapses. But again, I want to clarify that irrespective of the type of protocol, relapse can happen as cancer is not yet proved 100% curable.

In few cases of relapses, when we talked to the parents, we got to know that the cases were mostly for the patient with standard/intermediate protocols. High risk relapse cases are low as compared to standard/intermediate cases.

Consolidation phase treatment was similar to induction phase treatment. During the consolidation phase chart, he did got infections, cold, cough but got cured without getting admitted to the hospital.

But due to chemotherapy, the blood counts were suppressed. Every day we were in hospital since morning till evening because during this phase his platelets and hemoglobin was always down. I think total 7-8 times, the platelets transfusion happened and at least 2-3 times the blood transfusion happened. If the platelets are less than 15000 then chemotherapy can be given only after the platelet's transfusion. And if the hemoglobin is 7 or less, then the chemotherapy is given after the blood transfusion.

One big difference from induction phase was he was eating every two hours during induction and was always hungry, but during consolidation, he was having very very less meals. He stopped eating the way he was eating earlier. Sometimes in the whole day he was just having one forth chapati, 1/8th bowl of rice, very very less quantity. We tried to give him different types of food items, because eating is must during chemotherapy treatment. Before induction phase, when I checked with dietician, "should we avoid spices or oil"? then she clearly said for chemotherapy eating is must, you should put spice or oil otherwise the person going through chemotherapy will not be going to eat anything and eating is must. Only we should try to avoid outside food because it contains germs. At home whatever we are cooking we can give to child. She also told me if he is not eating, give him fritters but all homemade.

At the start of the consolidation phase, doctor told us that there would be mood swings so patiently we need to handle the child. And it was true, because during this phase I saw his fierce form, most of the time he was very angry. Chemotherapy impacted him so much that suddenly he was getting angry and frustrated and, in a moment, he starts crying.

He was behaving like we are enemy to him; his frustration level was on peak. He was not liking us and always say that I will not live with you guys, I will live with nana and Nani.

It was hard time for us to make him eat, every time, we were taking him in car and make him eat inside the moving car. Sometimes we were going to central park to make him eat, sometimes on mountains to make him eat, just to make him eat something. We almost took all actions which were needed in order to make him eat something. We were like, in whatever way he eats, let's do it otherwise dietician is certainly going to suggest for a nutrition pipe which is mostly unbearable for not only Arjun but for us too. Many kids during the second phase of treatment refuse to eat or lessen their diet, which results in low BMI index, so for most kids with low BMI, dietician suggests a nutrition pipe where feeding can be done through nose.

Though the nutrition pipe doesn't do any harm, instead the diet would be regular and it's a normal and an expected procedure, but still we wanted to escape from any type of surgery or something because not easy for Arjun at all. We cannot imagine our child with a nutrition pipe, so we tried all possible ways to make him eat a balanced diet though it can be of less quantity as compared to induction phase but still we successfully maintained his BMI index.

A very good thing about Arjun is, if I ask him not to eat chocolates, he will not eat, he is not very fond of eating chocolates, chips or any outside food except Pizza and French fries. But during whole treatment we did not take any risk of giving him any type of outside food.

Before the induction treatment was started, his phosphorus level was not good, so doctor suggested us that make sure he drinks lots of water during the treatment and after the treatment also, so the internal parts of body such as kidney works properly, because chemotherapy are harmful too, it has a long-lasting side effect. So, we made sure that he drinks a good amount of water every day.

Dietician always praised us that "the way you both are handling and taking care of your child is tremendous because his reports are normal and the BMI index also within range.

So finally, after 60 days, consolidation phase treatment also got over. And if you are a parent of a child who is suffering from cancer, you will feel the happiness after successfully completing each phase of treatment.

It feels like we have cleared one more roadblock from our path.

B-All Intense Maintenance High Risk

Again, a very very tough phase of treatment was the B-ALL Intense Maintenance treatment. This particular protocol is only for the high-risk category patient as the chemo is much intensive.

In this treatment, a patient needs to get admitted for 4 days and then the chemotherapy is given. And since it's an admit chemo, so it's the toughest job now to give chemotherapy to Arjun after admitting him.

As I mentioned earlier, Arjun don't have much problem with the outpatient procedure which means during the day only chemotherapy gets over. During the daytime processes it mostly takes just 2-3 hours for chemotherapy and if there is any blood transfusion then it might take some more hours, but anyways in evening we are mostly at our home.

For other children it might not be that tough because other children understand that only during the prick, we get hurts and after that they become habitual and friendly to the nurses, play also in hospital, but for Arjun it was like he don't want to be in hospital during night and due to which he cries a lot. He doesn't want to sleep on that hospital bed. We know that he is going to cry for the whole 4 days when he will be in hospital. Some people say make him mentally aware, but the case was not feasible for Arjun, if we try to make him mentally aware beforehand so he is going to cry from the day we tried to make him mentally aware so he will cry in advance only.

In this phase, there are four admit chemotherapies with a gap of 15 days between each chemotherapy.

So, after the first admit chemotherapies which consist of 4 days, the next chemotherapy would be after 15 days gap so kind of like 16 days in hospital which is very very difficult for Arjun.

This particular chemotherapy goes through veins and since it a very hard chemo medicine, it could impact skin also, if by mistake any single drop is spilled. It's a high dose of MTX.

Just for information I would like to mention Chemotherapies are given via veins (can be insertion of cannula or PICC) or orals or in muscles. It is also given in the spinal cord sometimes.

When the second phase got over and we went to the next OPD scheduled, the doctor asked us "Why there is no PICC line in Arjun's hand"?

PICC is a catherar tube made of silicon which is inserted into the vein of hand and it goes directly near the vein of heart. This was, I think specially made for pediatric patient, as once this tube gets inserted, so going forward only in case of blood test, there would be a prick, otherwise chemo, blood transfusion everything can me made possible through this tube.

With the help of this tube, nurses don't have to prick a child again and again and everything whether it's a chemo or transfusion can be made through this pipe, so the children don't get pricked/hurt again and again. Even if the nerves are not visible to the nurses, it is much easier to give chemotherapy through this pipe as compared to cannula. In cannula, a child is pricked again and again until a good vein is seen.

But the major drawback of the PICC catherar tube is, a proper care has to be taken for this tube. Every week dressing is required which makes children uncomfortable. And since PICC have more chances of getting infections, so without proper care and dressing it is quite risky to put in children hand. And since we were aware of this side effects as some parents previously told us, we preferred to have cannula over PICC in both the previous treatment charts. We were never in favor of PICC, but we were also not aware that PICC is must for the high-risk patient as this treatment phase has hard chemotherapy. We cannot give high doses of MTX chemo medicine through cannula as it may impact skin while in PICC it's safe. Since Arjun is a mild autistic and hyper active child, doctor suggested to have the PICC procedure through IR (Interventional Radiology) meaning by giving general anaesthesia, he can have PICC inserted. For other children, the PICC procedure is not that complex as they are given the local anaesthesia, but I have seen they also cry a lot as the pain is unbearable.

We took an appointment on 23rd October 2023 at 7 a.m., for the PICC procedure. Doctors suggested not to give him any solid food for 6 hours, he can only have appy juice or water 2 hours before the procedure. So, we did not give him any solid food after 12 midnight. In the morning 7:00 am we took him for the procedure, but the doctor came at 3:00 PM in afternoon, we were very angry that time, as doctor was so careless that he didn't even bother to tell us that you can give your child some food as the procedure is postponed to 3 PM. For a cancer patient, food is must and how he did not tell us to give food, we were waiting for him since morning and then from 12 midnight, entire day passed Arjun did not have anything. That time, we were cursing each other why we came to this hospital. Later we got to know that some emergency case came which the doctor was handling, so he got late, but then at least he should have called us. He only called us at night for the confirmation of procedure, so at least some decency should be maintained for pediatric patients to not keep them hungry.

That day was the worst day for us, as Arjun was crying like mad, as he was hungry plus after he was in sense, he saw the PICC got inserted in his hand. He was frustrated and was not able to tolerate. He was like, he is going to remove that pipe. And during that whole day, we were back to our initial days of diagnosis, "why my son god", "why not any of us". We are mature, we can tolerate things, but for children it's tough. "What sins we have made that we are going through this".

That day we also thought, why we are alive, it would have been better if me and my son would have died in some accident or something.

Doctor send him in recovery room and he was crying a lot, we told them that he will be fine once he reaches home, they were like, no, we need to see that oozing don't happen, and we knew that if he will be here, it will certainly happen but once he reaches home, he would be fine. We did not listen, we just asked nurse and then took him home at 5:30, gave him some food as he was very hungry. After eating, he was calm as he did not have anything since morning.

It was really a good luck for us, that after the first phase of treatment, he is now getting admitted directly in third chart of treatment.

Before making him to get admit for the chemotherapy, I lied and trying to convince him that in Kharghar where we lived during those days, is not our home, so we need to hand it our home to the owner for 4 days as they will celebrate their birthday there. They are going to hang balloons all over the walls. Since he is afraid of balloons, he was okay to be in hospital, but he said OKAY only in the home, after visiting hospital he did cry and told he is not going to stay in hospital. Before his admit chemotherapy started, I also took him to the "Little World Mall", Kharghar, where he purchased a lot of stationery items and total bill came was around Rs. 6000. We left it in car only, so that we will show him the products one by one while we are in hospital only, just to pass the 4 days in hospital. But, inspite of these things also he cried continuously in hospital, but when he realized the PICC is not hurting him he was little bit calm as compared to previous days, as now there is no more pricking in his hands.

And whichever type of children are, they will become calm after some days of treatment, it took little more for Arjun, as he is autistic, but then the children do understand that there are no options for them but to stay back in hospital and take the treatment.

And when you start staying in the pediatric ward, you will come to know, how many parents are losing hope each day and how much they are struggling for the extension of the life of their kids. It is very depressing and disheartening.

In the earlier two phases of treatment, we were just going to OPD's, taking chemotherapies in 3-4 hours and then coming back, so we did not see any deaths or neither heard the discussion between doctor and the parents who are grieving for the few more months of life of their child. These things we came to knew after we started staying in hospital for admit chemotherapies. We have seen deaths of some child patients of 1 year old, 10-year-old, 13-year-old teenager. Sometimes you will find a parent telling people that their child will be able to live for few months or weeks only, as doctor told. It's so hard to hear this, just imagine the situation of a parent there. It's so sad and disheartening to feel all this. Those days, we realized life is not same for all the parents. Few patients only get cured and some parents has to go through all this.

During every admit chemo's we hear few such cases. I remember one incident, there was a 13-year-old teenager boy, the doctor already told his parents that chances are very less, as the cancer cells are spread everywhere but we will try. Sister's always keep on saying that he is very naughty, annoying and shout a lot and Arjun also shouts and cry a lot so let's have their bed side by side, so other children can sleep peacefully. So after sometime, his bed was moved next to Arjun's bed. I asked that boy, "How are you". He replied "I am absolutely fine aunty; I don't know why my parents brought me here. I want to go

Uncertainty: The Painful Experience

home". Looking at him even I thought he is absolutely fine, may be sister's perception was different from me. He was very polite by nature.

But when the night came and everyone was sleeping, he was crying loudly due to unbearable pain, which nobody could understand other than him, he was repeatedly telling his mom to take him home. That time I realized that how emotionless that sister was. She was saying him annoying, naughty and all, but actually due to that unbearable pain he was crying. Since, in admit chemotherapies, we have to stay for 4 days, so within these four days, that boy's mother became like a friend. She showed me some paintings he made. It was so beautiful I cannot express. He was very fond of making Ganesh pictures. He also made few plans for Ganesh Chaturthi for 2024, which he was telling me and inviting me to his home.

Since before getting admitted, we purchased few stationery items for Arjun which included some permanent colorful marker pens. He requested me to share some pens with him also, so I gave him. He returned back to me during Arjun's discharge from hospital, the 4th day of the admit chemotherapy and told me, "Next time when you come, please buy some marker pen for me also and my father is going to give you the money", I smiled at him seeing his decency that he was like I will purchase from you, I will not take it for free. I told him OKAY next time I will bring for you.

I just liked that teenage boy so much that, as soon as I got time, I went to the same "Little world Mall", to bought him the similar type of marker, even I also purchased a new type of marker which is called a floating marker, so after drawing something on the backside of spoon with the floating marker and then, if we keep that spoon in water, that drawing which we have drawn on spoon will float in the water.

I thought once we will go for the second admit chemotherapy, I will ask my husband to call his dad and give that marker pen to his son.

So, while preparing for the 2nd admit chemotherapy when we went to hospital, my husband called his dad. His dad picked up the phone and told us that he is no more and started crying. We were shocked and devastated. I have that inner guilt that after purchasing why I did not give him as soon as I purchased, he would have been happy, I wanted to see that happiness on his face. A teenage boy so attached to Ganesa, making plans for next year, making Ganesha painting, and what Ganesha gave him was so much pain that he can't even slept peacefully during his last days. I think after 4-5 days only he got expired after last I talked to him. It's a lifetime sorrow for the parents. Since such incident I faced for the first time, I cried for 2 days remembering him again and again. I think this happened sometime between 20 to 26 November and I don't know the guilt I was having; I am not able to overcome it.

We have to now focus now on Arjun's second chemotherapy, so we went ahead, tried to forget the previous incident. During our second visit for admit chemotherapy, we saw a child who was perfectly fine, but the case was of cancer relapse. He was absolutely fine, but due to the chemotherapy side-effects, he lost his vision.

Just imagine a child who was a healthy boy, doing his daily routine work, going to school also, playing, doing everything a healthy child does and then within few days, he lost his vision, and imagine how he is going to feel now. His father was telling every day he cries and say why am I living, I want to die. Just imagine for almost 3 years, his treatment was going on, now again the cancer got relapsed, plus he lost his vision also due to chemotherapy side effects.

During the third admit chemo's sessions, we met a very good and a jolly parent who were from same area where my in-laws live, i.e., Balihar, Buxar. Every time they try to be jolly, pulling legs or do some comedy talk. Those days we sometimes forget also our bad days.

Those jolly parents were already told by the doctor that their son is not going to survive for more than 1 months. It was because, even after multiple surgeries, the brain tumor was still there. And the parents of that 2-year-old child just requesting the doctor to continue the antibiotic so she can survive for few more days.

I cannot hold my tears and asked the mother of that child, she seems to be jolly, but as soon as I asked her, she burst out in tears. The parents were trying to be jolly and smiling but deep inside, their heart was crying continuously.

One interview of Rajpal Yadav with Lallaantop was viral where when asked about which were the tough days of him. He replied, we think these are the tough days where you don't earn, but once visiting Tata Hospital, he actually came to know about the tough days, where people are sleeping outside on roads to get the treatment. They lose their jobs due to this treatment. There are parents whose child or relatives suffering and how they are feeling. He said after seeing those people, he came to know that his suffering is very very less as compared to these people so we must thank God for that.

After some days, the 4th admit chemotherapy also got over successfully and finally the 3rd chart also got over. We were happy that now no more stay in hospital.

My parents went to their hometown after the first admit chemo, we thought we will be able to manage it. And we were able to manage without them. They were not going, but I only thought that at least they should visit the house once, they are old so they also need some days to relax. But after four five days, it was becoming difficult to manage without them, so we discussed and decided that this time we can call my in-laws for few days. My mother is law also is super active at the age of 70, just like my mother. I feel very lucky that my parents as well as my mother-in-law both are active at the age of 70. My father-in-law is also good but he is much older now so we cannot rely on him for anything at this situation.

We got the reservation confirmed on 6 November 2023 and my parents went to hometown on 31st October 2023. Now after my mother-in-law came, she took care of the things which my mom was doing previously. Before the treatment only we decided we will not keep maid as if any outside people coming to home can be the medium of infection. So, me and my husband was doing sweeping, washing clothes, washing utensils along with our job. And sweeping we were doing two times in a day as there was lot of pigeons coming in balcony.

After some days, when Dec month started, my in-laws started getting multiple calls from home, so later we thought that might be people there require them more, so we decided to send them to hometown. We got the reservation confirmed for their return on 3rd January 2024.

Just wanted to add that third chart went smoothly, there was no fever, no cough, no infections during this phase. Arjun was absolutely fine. Even his blood counts were perfect, no platelets or blood transfusion was done in these phases as the counts were all good. He also gained little weight and he was eating properly. My birthday was on 23rd December and Arjun was waiting eagerly as we promised him to give him cake. He did not had any outside items during the entire treatment. We made sure that he did not eat any type of food items containing sugar, but since he was craving badly for cake, we gave him little bit of cake on my birthday. I did not wanted to celebrate my birthday in 2023, but since he was eagerly waiting, I thought not to dishearten him. That happiness I saw on his face first time during the treatment. He missed Ganesh Chaturthi and Garba during Navratri, every time he was going on the window to see, whenever the music started for Garba. He was also watching from the balcony only Ganpati visarjan. Those time we really felt bad, that what god gave him, that he is not able to enjoy now. So, he really enjoyed my birthday, though we did not went outside, but he enjoyed the cake cutting also.

B-All High Risk Intensification

We thought that after the third phase of admit chemotherapies, we will get some relax and now there would not be any more admits.

But it turned out to be quite opposite. This phase turned out to be the hardest of all the previous phases. This phase chart was the combination of first and second phase chart i.e., combination doses of first chart and second chart. One new steroid tablet added in this chart which was very very hard, it brings down the ANC (Absolute Neutrophils Count) and this causes infections, so the patient is more prone to infections.

As I previously mentioned, with PICC tube, there is a high risk of infection and unfortunately due to PICC, Arjun got infections.

It was on 1st January 2024; we got an appointment of PICC dressing. Since it was holiday and the staffs were very less. At 3:00 pm we visited for PICC dressing to the clinical room, as we were told to come at 3.00 pm on 1st Jan 2024. The staffs were in hurry and were about to leave due to holiday. Because they were in hurry, they missed few protocols which get followed during dressing PICC. She forgot to put a disposable napkin below the hands before doing the dressing. We told her that time, that you missed to keep the disposable napkin to which she said nothing will happen don't worry. We thought since she is a nurse she would know more. I think except her, all staffs follow the protocol, maybe she also follows but in hurry she skipped that. In ACTREC, all staffs are very punctual and strictly adhere to protocols. Sometimes they even scold us if any mistake is done from our side. And this was a miss, my son got fever of 101 degree in night, we rushed to casualty. We told the nursing staff that in the evening the dressing was done without keeping that disposable napkin, maybe it could be the reason. They said "Yes" during dressing sometimes infections do occur and that could be the reason of fever but don't worry, that bacteria are not that much serious. He again have to undergo all the tests CBC, CRP, Blood culture. After few days when the blood culture report came it was positive. Doctor called us and told us don't worry it's just a skin infection which is mostly caused during the nursing procedure when one's bacteria enters the skin of another person whose immunity is suppressed. We were worried but hopefully after giving the antibiotic in vein every 12 hours, he was absolutely fine after 3 days.

The chemotherapy of the fourth chart was not started on the required date due to fever, but once the fever was gone, doctor asked to go for chemotherapy as per forth chart.

His fourth chart was on track, getting chemotherapies on planned dates, we also started making plans for going to Pune. We were very very excited going back to our home in Pune. The chart was of 49 days, out of which 39 days successfully passed without any infections or fever. We were like, only 10 days remaining now and then doctor will allow us to go to Pune now and will put the next chart. Life again would be on track when we will reach Pune, we were very very excited, even Arjun also.

But then again, he got fever of temperature 102 degrees, we rushed to casualty, undergone same tests which they normally suggest CRP, CBC and Blood culture test. This time the fever was not coming down even after 5 days course of antibiotics. The temperature was between 102 to 100.6 always, it was not coming to low grade fever. When the blood culture report came it showed a gram-negative bacterium which is very harmful and sometimes life taking. It was the seventh day of the fever and still the temperature was not coming down, immediately doctor said to admit him. And then the doctor started the fever treatment from low to high doses of antibiotics. Now since his immunity was already suppressed, and the ANC was very very low, he caught mouth sore also and it became hard for him to eat anything. He was unable to eat anything and with a high-grade fever, we were so much worried that what is going to happen now. The dietician was called to recommend how to keep the intake of food, as he was having mouth sore. The dietician suggested to give TPM, which is a bag just like the bag of blood and platelets and it was to be given through veins. TPM bag contains all the necessary minerals /vitamins which are needed for the body. I don't know whether in other cancer hospitals, these things are being focused or not, but that time, I was like what would have happened suppose if took the treatment from any other hospitals. In Tata, every minute details are kept in mind, whether it's a infection control department or nutrition department or our nursing staff. It was a very very tough time for us, but nursing staff always calming us down that this is expected don't worry, it happens mostly to children as their immunity is suppressed, he will be fine within few days.

Before the treatment began, when I showed the bone marrow report to my office boss, I told him that the treatment will get over in 6 months because this is what I thought. After the treatment started, I came to know that the treatment will take a minimum of 8-9 months as there comes a lot of complications in between. Sometimes it gets delayed due to infections, sometimes it gets delayed due to low blood count.

Chemotherapy is not given in case of ANC count low or platelets is less or any infections or fever is there. Sometimes my boss calls me up to ask for Arjun health, I felt myself as so lucky to part of the team who's main focus was always health. Since my boss was unaware that the treatment lasts long and he thought to help me out to cope up with the office task after a long gap. Though I was part of a team, but he never assigned me any task which have a deadline. He always assigns me task which I can do whenever I get sometime. He was worried about the gaps I had as I was in a non- billable code, so he assigned me a billable project code. If a person is in billable project code the chances of layoffs is less. A person with a non-billable project code would be the first, if the layoffs happen. So, in January 2024, he assigned me on a billable project code, but I was finding little difficult to manage as anytime I have to rush to hospital and this will not show a good rapport/impression on client due to non-availability in working hours. So again, I informed him that it is not possible to support client project due to uncertainties. He agreed and said to me "Priyanka, I was not aware of this, please focus on Arjun's treatment for now, we will check and update you". He is director in my organization, 4 levels up from my designation, but still he understands and calls whenever needed. I am so much grateful/thankful to him. I worked in three Multinational organization, but I have never seen such a manager/supervisor who are so much helpful and understands the situation.

We were in hospital for almost 8 days from 26th Jan 2024 to 2nd Feb 2024 and later when the report came, the infection found out to be in a PICC line. Doctors asked us what to do now, to put a new PICC line or continue with cannula. Without thinking for a second, we said cannula. It's okay he will cry but infections causing more health issues. We were okay with cannula as it has less chances of infection and we don't have to come for regular dressing which is prone to infections. I was so much tensed during those days, as my parents were also in hometown and we were alone, me, my husband and my son. On the first day of admission when we were in hospital to admit Arjun for fever, my father called me and as soon as he asked how is Arjun, I burst out in tears because I was so worried of fever with mouth sore. I told him about this and the very next day my parents came. After they came there was a hope and a positivity. During this time, the mental peace is also very important and family is one of the which gives you support and mental peace. My father was so calm during those times, he said you are worrying unnecessarily, Arjun will be alright soon. He told me now we will not go anywhere until Arjun's treatment gets over. Every day I remember them and think what would have happened if they were not with me during those times.

Even the doctor was so much worried and tensed when Arjun fever was not coming down. And when his fever came low, she was having a very broad smile on her face. She felt relaxed and she also seems happy after Arjun's was fine. Every pediatric oncologist doctor in TMH and ACTREC is emotionally attached to the patient. I have never seen such doctors anywhere in other hospitals. In tata hospitals, you will also see the doctors are available 24x7, unlike other hospitals. Sometimes, I have seen some pediatric doctors doing overtime, sleep for just 3-4 hours, anytime they are being called by pediatric staffs. And everyone can see their workload through their eyes, sometimes their eyes are red. Sometimes even doctors are not feeling well, can be seen on their faces, but still they come to hospitals regular basis. There daily routine is like first around 8-9 a.m. in the morning they will visit pediatric wards to see the admit patients, then they come to OPD from 9 a.m-5 p.m., sometimes stays more, then go back to their PG's/hostel and again came back at around 6.30 p.m. and stays back till night. And unlike other doctors they will not get frustrated if you ask something. Anytime if you are asking anything to pediatric doctors, they are going to reply with patience.

Even the nursing staffs are so good here, they are always going to show you a happy gesture, so the patients are very comfortable with them. Not a single line of frustration could be seen on their faces, always showing a smiling face. I have seen many senior patients talking very very rudely to nursing staff and that is expected because with this disease, a patient become depressed, he/she sometimes suffers from anxiety and nursing staff understand these scenarios, they are very very polite with the patients. They are also very well- trained and never take risk with the patients. I felt that when sometimes they see the file and some doubts or any issues is there, or they are not understanding anything, they are first going to call a doctor or directly go to the doctor clears the issues/doubts, then only they will proceed with chemotherapy.

So finally, the most awaited moment came for us, the fourth chart also got over successfully and doctor told us after 15 days once the counts are all back to normal, they will give us release from Tata hospital and we can move to Pune.

It almost took one more month for us, for attaching the Maintenance chart i.e., last chart for Arjun as his ANC was very low. Though it was increasing but at a very slow rate. So finally on 11 March, we visited Pune once the counts were normal, but we still did not let our Kharghar flat owner to know that we were vacating the flat, as we were ourself not sure, whether we should stay in Kharghar only for 2 more years or we should move back to Pune.

But after coming to Pune, we got a mental peace which was much needed for all three of us.

Doctor suggested to take care of him very well, to avoid any outside food, make a healthy habit for him and he also suggested to make him go to school.

Behavioural Therapy Sessions In Actrec

A cancer patient goes through various stages of ups and downs. Due to this hard treatment and various ups and downs, sometimes the patient goes through depression. Sometimes in case of Arjun and may be in other kids as well, the fear of injections is set deeply in their mind, sometimes Arjun wakes up suddenly during the sleep with lot of fear of injections, as if dreaming about injections only. Being autistic, Arjun is one of those children who have lot of fear of injections even after knowing, he has to go through all this. Other children become habitual after 2 or 3 pricks, they cry for 2-3 days or maximum till 15 days, but after some days they get adjusted and become habitual. Everyone in the hospital, whether the other parents or nursing staff or doctors were very surprised that till date how he is not getting adapted to injections or pricks.

So, during the second phase of treatment due to his excessive crying and not supporting nursing staffs, doctor suggested some occupational and behavioral therapy for Arjun. The therapy sessions were free of cost and the therapist doctor was so well trained and a good human being.

She started some sessions with Arjun. Initially Arjun resisted to go for session, but later when he came to know that the sessions are just for playing, he was very happy. He really loved that doctor who was taking the therapy sessions. After few sessions, she said that you should be very proud parents. She told us that she observed him in some sessions and came to conclusions that Arjun is having savant skills. She mentioned the details in the file. Savant meaning is God gifted skills, she told us that she was shocked to see how quickly her memories and visualize things. It is much faster than the other children. We were already aware, but we thought that it is due to being autistic, he got that quality to visualize and memorize faster than others. Even in his schools, his teachers always say us, "Arjun is little naughty, he will open/shut the door, on/off the switches, press the lift buttons, but in terms of academics, if other children will take 1 week for studying 2 chapters, Arjun will need only a day." When we informed his teachers about the disease, they told us not to worry at all, just focus on the treatment and his health and anyways Arjun have a sharp mind, he can complete whole syllabus in just 1 or 2 weeks. I know he is intelligent; he can recite tables from 1 to 40 without a break. Sometimes he recited table of 28, 29 Infront of doctors also, so one of the senior doctors also said that "When Arjun is coming to OPD, don't use calculators, just ask Arjun as he is our calculator". They were surprized to see how good he is with numbers.

The therapy doctor was always writing good things about him. He always answers all her questions. Though he is sharp minded, but only thing is he is not socialised. Now a days he do the physical activities also, but earlier he was not doing any physical activity.

The therapy doctor took 3-4 sessions in a week and it really helped him to mix-up with some sisters and brothers. He started liking the Tata hospital and he is not afraid now, even gives smiles to doctors now and slowly got comfortable with most staffs.

Maintenance Treatment Chart For 2 Years

Currently Arjun's 3rd Maintenance chart is going on. There would be a total 8 maintenance chart for 2 years. Each maintenance chart is of 84 days i.e., approx. 3 months. So, we need to go to ACTREC Kharghar for every 3 months now. It is little bit scaring for Arjun, because he thinks the treatment is over, but every 3 months this chemotherapy is given through intrathecal meaning on the spinal cord which is very painful. And giving injection on the backbone is very painful for him, he doesn't support the doctors and many times, they were like we will not be able to give him as he is rotating his back continuously. Sometimes, this chemotherapy is given to him after giving pediatric sleeping syrup, sometimes it's given after giving him anesthesia, as he never supported, whereas for other children, they don't need sleeping pills or anaesthesia, though they cry but they don't move their body. And this chemo which is called MTX through intrathecal i.e., through the back side bone can only be given by oncologist doctors. It is not given by nursing staffs. So not only Arjun, we are also afraid when that time comes. On 5th Dec 2024, 4th maintenance will get attached. We only think that Arjun should be a survivor, we think all the 8 charts should be successful and he should be declared cancer free after that.

Uncertainty: The Painful Experience

Travelling back to Pune from Kharghar was altogether a new adventure for us. We were very very happy, that we are going to meet our friends after so long. Arjun will meet his teachers, his principal maam.

When the First chart of maintenance was attached from March to May, we decided to visit Tata hospital every 15 days, though the doctor said that now you can move to Pune and come every 3 months. But still we thought that lets tell them that during first chart of maintenance we need a regular follow-up so we want to visit every 15 days as we were also afraid about the side effects of chemotherapies. A regular visit will satisfy us that everything is alright now and we can monitor him closely.

But actually, it turned out to be vice-versa of what we thought. Later on, we realized that it's not feasible to visit Kharghar from Pune every 15 days. We are creating it hectic for Arjun as well as for us. Travelling itself for 6 hours in a day is a challenge so we were taking Airbnb rooms whose per day cost is around 3000-4000 Rs, plus we are impacting our office work also and this 7-hour journey we are doing from the car every 15 days is making Arjun more prone/risk to infections plus car is not that much comfortable. Doctors always suggest to come in three months unless there is any emergency or fever or there is any problem with the patient.

Sometimes, we sent him to school for class test, but now we are not sending him due to lot of dengue, malaria and viral cases. Slowly, all three of us me, Arjun and my husband are trying to move on, leaving behind the old days, bad memories, the days we struggled, the pain my son went through.

We are lucky that the school in which Arjun is studying is supporting us in all possible ways, no burden or any type of loads of his studies. We also don't make him study like other kids. We are like if he wants, he will study, if not then it's okay.

At the same time, we were also worried about catching of infections if we send him school.

Sometimes, because of chemotherapies side effects, he have difficulty in walking, he starts limping. Due to chemotherapies, there are certain deficiencies also, which we are trying to cover by giving him as many fruits, nuts etc. we can.

Recently after seeing so many relapse cases, we talked about it to his school principal ma'am, we thought that these two years till 2026, we will be only sending him to school for class test or exam or either we can send him for an hour only, so that he don't get bored sitting at home.

But now, we are not sending him, teaching him at home only. Once he gets fully recovered, after 2 years we will send him in full fledge.

In the maintenance chart, the chemo still happens, but unlike we don't have to visit hospital. There are oral MTX doses once a week, and daily there is a 6 MP tablet.

The doses depend on the weight, age and height of the child and the ANC counts. And every 3 months the chemo injection is given in backbone. So, the chemotherapy, we can say still going on, but it's taken orally. Till now, the counts and everything is fine, sometimes problem still arise in his legs, he starts limping and get tired most often.

Arjun's Sixth Birthday

I decided to write the journey what my son and we have gone through after his 6th birthday, so here I am. I thought of sharing my experiences with the people I know through the medium of my book.

23rd April 2024, my son's sixth birthday came, we were in Pune and thrilled and thankful that his 9 months treatment got over before his birthday. Though we came to Pune, but never thought of going to any malls, as earlier we were like every weekend being spent in malls only. And since it's been a year since Arjun last visited Pune malls, Arjun was excited that today on his birthday he will go to mall. Earlier, since he was visiting on regular basis, he don't have that craving kind of feeling for anything. Now he was craving for going mall, eating French fries.

So, this year, we planned to go to Season's mall, Pune and entire day we were in mall, we took some food items for Arjun along with us.

We took him to his favorite play station i.e., Time Zone where he spends almost whole day playing games. He was very very excited and happy that day and we were emotional and happy to see him like this as he was before. Then we took him to Mc Donald's as he was craving for French fries. That day was kind of cheat day for him. He did not had French fries since 1 year. We usually avoid to give him any type of outside food or junk food. Only French fries is an outside food which he had sometimes, otherwise everything we give him home made and freshly cooked. Before 1 year, we were having mostly outside food and we were giving him also, not realizing that outside food habits can impact his health. And that time he was not at all interested in outside food as he was eating on regular basis, but now since it's been a year he ate any outside food, so he craves for it.

But I must say he is not at all obstinate, if I tell him not to eat, he will not eat. He never asks us for chocolate, chips or anything, so we feel lucky that he himself don't get craving of these items.

In evening when we came back from Seasons mall, I ordered a cake for him. He was very excited to see the cake and he ate the cake, but I told him that it's sweets are harmful for health, so let's take in small quantity. He followed and ate in a less quantity. This birthday was very special for us. We have mixed feelings, we really felt happy for him. He was also very happy.

May-July Fearful Month

May to July month, every year, we faced some challenges in Arjun's health, so every year, we are like, these three months May, June, July is the hardest months for us, so it should pass quickly.

In 2022, my son got dengue during these months, and in last year 2023, he got diagnosed with blood cancer.

May to July month is always a very depressing month for us. This year too, it was depressing, I heard a very disappointing news on 13th May which was the road accident of my office boss's one and only son.

I was so disappointed and mentally disturbed that my every minute every second got spends remembering him. That accident was like revolving around my senses again and again.

After I heard the news, I didn't have words to console him, just messaged him on whatsapp and did not called him. I was sure that I will not be able to call him, don't know why I felt guilty.

Even I never called him after that neither I pinged him on office network. I don't know why; I am feeling guilty of messaging him also.

My office boss helped me so much during Arjun's treatment, and every day me and my whole family including my mother and father gave him blessings that his family should always be happy and live long life. I am still in guilt that I could not do anything for him.

Once he visited Pune office in March, I went to meet him in office, to see him in-person and invite him and his family for dinner. I messaged him next time when you visit Pune please come with family and have dinner with us. He was like sure next time I will come for sure. Then on 13th May 2024, this news came. I was like "What type of Karma result is this". He is so good, down to earth person, always advice to take care of family first, as family health comes first, and suddenly God took the life of his only son.

Where are those blessings which not only us but I think whole team gives him for being so good person. Certainly God did not do good with him. His son was 21 years only and after living for almost 21 years together with his mother and dad, suddenly he met with accident. How the parents are going to live without him.

So today is the time, I am neither believing in God nor any type of Karma.

In July month only, one of our Tata hospital friend's son leukemia got relapsed and when the visited tata hospital, the doctors told that chances are very less and he will be able to survive for few months only. Recently, on Dussehra, he got expired. When I talked to his parents, they told that he was very happy when he went see the Durga Pandal on Navami day, but soon after he came back home, he caught fever and he did not woke after that. On his last day, his parents asked him, "Are you going to leave us son? Please don't go. We will not be able to live without you". He cried a lot that day and after sometime in afternoon, he closed his eyes on his mother's lap. Till today, I miss him. He was so supportive during the treatment, sometimes he also tells Arjun that see you should not cry, I also don't cry. Till today, the parents are unable to move on, they always cry whenever I call them. He was of same age as Arjun, his birthday falls on 11 may and Arjun birthday falls on 23rd April. Arjun is some days older than him.

Arjun, "The Warrior"

Yes, my son "Arjun" is also a warrior same like "Arjun" in the epic "Mahabharata". He have all the qualities of the warrior "Arjun" in Mahabharata. He have the skills like 'the concentration power' which we can see in the lead character Arjuna of Mahabharata. As Arjuna was able to string a heavy bow and hit the eye of the rotating fish, by just looking at the reflection in the pool of water. I have observed my son also have a good concentration skills. He also have intelligent mind just like Arjuna in Mahabharata. And as Arjuna in Mahabharata fight till end with Kaurava, I know my son is also going to fight with cancer and surely wins the battle. He is very strong and I firmly believe he will be the winner.

Most parents who took their child's treatment from tata hospital are in contact with each other and we are also in connect with them.

And it's like once a month we hear some bad news either the cancer got relapsed or the doctor already told no more possibility of survival. And most of our days being spent either being depressed or disturbed. But still, we try to move on every day after seeing my son. We always try to be very happy Infront of him, so he don't gets idea that what disease he is having. We just have told him, every kid sometimes have fever and they have to go through all this, so it's not only you, even we also have gone through this when we were small.

Each day when he wakes up happily, we are so happy. Earlier we don't give hug to each other but after all this happened, we regularly give hug to each other. Arjun being in the middle of me and his father. We tightly hug him kiss him, cuddle him and he also kisses and hugs us every time. It's like every day is a blessing to us seeing him happy. Since he is born, every day we spent half an hour kissing him, cuddling him as soon as he wakes up. We spend most hours with each other, sometimes go to mountains, sometimes, put a loud music at home sing and dance.

After going through all this, today we are like let's enjoy every moment of life, because life is very uncertain, you never know when we will stop breathing. And with this incident, we also understood how important is to spend time with family. I cannot live a single moment without seeing Arjun or his father. Arjun is my heart and I cannot survive without my heart.

Some of my friends suggest me to plan a second baby, but I think I cannot give Arjun's love to anyone else.

I also want to mention about my society friends here. Earlier when we returned back to Pune, though we felt a bit of relax and soothing surroundings, but still we have mental stress, sometimes it's because of disease sometimes it was a office work pressure, sometimes it's related with house works, sometimes it was like how to face the world, but then when I met my society friends, they told me "Priyanka sometimes you should come out of your home and try to take a walk in evening with us". I have not talked much to them earlier, I was having only my best friend to talk, but as she also have kid, office and then other works, so thought of not disturbing her. But I know she will be always available for me inspite of having so much workload. And I literally realized, how important is friends. Now I go for a walk daily, talk with them and try to move on with life. I know they all are aware about my situations and understand.

Small Request/Urge To Everyone Reading This

When my son's Leukemia was diagnosed, I only told my best friend of college who live in my society only, about the disease. I would have told to people, but I was not in a situation that time. And I also hide it, because few people might have the mindset that cancer is an infectious disease.

But in Feb 2024, an incident happened after which I felt very guilty and regretful that why I have not informed about this to at least my close friends.

We have a group of some close friends from my previous organization, Amdocs, and I did not inform them about it. Whenever they were calling me, I was telling them Arjun is fine and we are in our hometown.

Later on, somewhere in Feb 2024, one of my Amdocs friend's daughter was having her birthday, I wished her. That friend is mostly away from social media, but on her birthday, she put the photo of her child, so I wished her and we have some nice chats as I was also happy that now Arjun's treatment is all over in the end of February and soon, we will be meeting in Pune.

Suddenly after a week only I got a call from my other Amdocs friend of same close friends' group. I avoided her call as I was in hospital at that time and thought that I will call her once I reach home and we will chat and make some good plans now. Then she messaged me "It's urgent", please call me as soon as possible". I was very worried. As soon as I reached, first thing I did was calling her. With a very very low voice she told me, our friend's daughter who was having the birthday on Feb last week is in very serious condition, she is in ICU.

I was shocked, what would have happened. But still, I have that faith that nothing will happen, she will be fine soon.

I waited for the next day to come so I can call my friend to ask for her daughter's health. As soon as I called her, she was crying and told me "Just pray for my daughter to your god, she is having multiple organ failure". After that she hanged up and I also did not call her as thought not to disturb her and just focus on her daughter for now. When I called my other friend, I came to knew that she was having viral pneumonia infection which led to multiple organ failure. On first week of March 2024, I got the news that she expired after fighting with the disease. After few days, I called my friend and told about my case also, I told her as soon as I am in Pune, I will be at your home, you don't worry and be brave. After having some discussion with her, she told the same symptoms which we experienced during the diagnosis of leukemia, but did not told her, as she have lost her child and I should not be asking much. She told me that on her birthday, she ate a cake, may be some infection was developed and after some time she became very very dull, she was not even standing and having any meal. So, they rushed to hospital and after checkup it was found a viral pneumonia with multiple organ failure. She cried a lot and I also cried a lot on phone. When she heard of Arjun, she was consoling me and cried why all this happened to us.

Later on, I felt very guilty that if I would have told about Arjun leukemia, they would have been more meticulous, more alerted and may be her life would have saved or at least would have survived more.

When I heard news of my boss's son accident, I thought at least I have got the opportunity to make my child recover, to make him healthy, at least I am aware of the disease. But just think about the parents who suddenly lost their child in an accident. The situation is like "Everything is going good in the morning, we are greeting each other and suddenly you come to know that your family member you greeted in the morning, now you will not be able to see him or hear him anymore as he is no more now.

In both the cases, the parents suffers as they lost their child and it's very very hard to accept the fact that you will not be able to see that child again.

So, I just want to request everyone that even if a small fever you or your child have, just go ahead with the CBC test. This is a very important test and now a days, many children have suffered from this. Whenever you do CBC test, just keep an eye on the Hemoglobin, platelets and white blood cells counts. WBC is the type of blood which is responsible for our immunity, so it should not be more than normal range or less than normal range. And if you see any deviation, just go to doctor immediately and ask for his advice. CBC i.e., complete blood count is a test that should be done on regular basis whether there is a fever or not.

Now a days the cancer is also becoming a common disease, as our way of living is so much changed as compared to the lives we were living earlier. Earlier we were having healthy food from home, now with the online food delivery apps, we were ordering the food from outside. Certain chemicals are being used in every food item we are eating and the chemicals are also responsible to cause cancer.

Also, I want to let everyone know that some cancers are genetic, so if any of your ancestors had the cancer, please take out some time and try to do a full body checkup every six months.

Also, sometimes we are not aware how our ancestors died because that time, very rarely the people were going to hospitals. It can be due to cancer, now a days with the advancement of medical science, we come to know about disease, but earlier going to hospital was not only a big challenge, but also people think about the money as the salary were less those days.

I have seen those bad days and I don't want anyone else to face the same days, so please do not wait until it's too late. I know every time it is not cancer, but with a regular CBC, you can monitor your health, eat as per the CBC report.

Earlier we rarely hear the cancer cases and usually it was caused to old people, but now a days the cancer cases are increasing with a fast rate. Earlier it was rare and most patients were old, but now small children, adolescence and people below 45 years are also getting cancer and the patient graph is increasing with a high rate. Everything have chemical in it, so before eating anything such as fruits or vegetables please make sure you wash it in warm water. In today's world, people first priority is business, so to make profit, manufacturers try to produce any item in a large quantity even if their production is less. And if the quantity is more but the production is less so anyways quality will hamper and they are going to mix some chemicals in the item. In this line I have used item as a commodity and it can be anything which you can think of. It can be medicines, it can be food items, it can be our fruits and vegetables. Every day we hear such news, sometimes it is some fake/duplicate drugs, sometimes we get milk mixing the shampoo in it, sometimes cabbage/egg is made of plastic substances. And this impacts severely to our health.

Recently I heard a famous youtuber Surbhi Jain died of ovary cancer, Hina Khan diagnosed with stage 3 breast cancer, Chavi Mittal was having breast cancer, Bihar leader Sushil Modi died of cancer then Sharda Sinha, a famous Bhojpuri singer, the list is long. These are celebrities we know, but there are many people including children who are struggling each day with cancer whom we don't know. It's a deadly disease, so I just want to urge you all, please do a regular body checkup and it's important. Cancer can happen to anyone; I have seen a 7-year-old boy having mouth cancer.

He never had any tobaccos or drinks or cigarette but still he is struggling with mouth cancer. An agarbatti, cigarette, smoke from burning tires or any type of smoke which we are inhaling are poisonous to our health.

Arjun's Daily Diet

Though we are aware that relapse can happen anytime. Relapse meaning is coming back of the cancer cells and its symptoms are same as cancer diagnosed for the first time.

Till today, my son's CBC report is normal, but since it's a cancer, cannot guarantee.

We take care of him very well. Give him the medicines on timely basis, not a single day have come when we have forgot the medicines. And I know, every parents are punctual with their child's health. As a parents, we become careless if we have to take care of ourselves, our medicines, but not in case of child. Every parent is super active when it comes to children health.

We also try to maintain all the healthy habits for him. Here are some, I want to share with you all.

As soon as he wakes up, we cuddle him and then give him 1 glass of warm water, sometimes we also give him normal water from RO. After 5-10 minutes he brushes his teeth. Then comes the breakfast. In breakfast we try that repetition should be less, so every day we make something different. On Saturday we give him poha, other days we give him sometimes Sooji uttapam, sometimes chapati and sabji, sometimes methi or palak paratha with chutney. We make sure that he should have methi (fenugreek), palak(spinach), paneer or garlic, or sometimes beans or chickpeas should be included in his breakfast as these are rich sources of folate and vitamins. He still eats less as compared to his age, he eats only 1 or 1 and half chapati, but we make sure he eats healthy whatever quantity he eats.

Later on, after breakfast, he go on the ground for an hour and do some physical activities with his father. It can be walking or cycling or jumping anything.

Once he comes back home after doing physical activities, we give him little bit of each berry kind of fruits. For example: two strawberry, three blueberries, two cherries, sometimes raspberry if available along with 1/8 of ripped papaya. Raspberry and mulberries he don't like the taste so we don't give him, but anytime if blueberries or cherries are out of stock in market and raspberry is available so we make him eat raspberry.

After having berry kind of fruits, he takes bath, study little bit, play with toys at home, then comes the lunch time.

In lunch we give him daal/pulse in which we put beetroot, raw papaya, gooseberry, Hing, turmeric and raw banana and it's my personal experience that if you are making daal like this, it will surely result in good hemoglobin, platelets and WBC count. Beetroot is good for hemoglobin, raw papaya and raw banana for platelets and gooseberry is good for immunity. We give him daal, rice and sabji or chutney in lunch. Sometimes, daal can be skipped if we make chole or rajma.

After lunch we make sure to give him lots of water so he can have good potty daily. Water helps in smooth functioning of kidney.

www.ingramcontent.com/pod-product-compliance
Lightning Source LLC
LaVergne TN
LVHW061555070526
838199LV00077B/7061